CHINESE COOKING
CANTONESE

INTERNATIONAL GOURMET

CHINESE COOKING
CANTONESE

Margaret Leeming

CRESCENT BOOKS
NEW YORK

First published in Great Britain in 1986 by
Ward Lock Limited, 8 Clifford Street, London
W1X 1RB, an Egmont Company.

This 1986 edition published by Crescent
Books, distributed by Crown Publishers, Inc.

Designed by Melissa Orrom.
Text filmset in Garamond Original by
M & R Computerised Typesetting Ltd.,
Grimsby.

Printed and bound in Portugal

h g f e d c b a

CONTENTS

Acknowledgements

Inside photographs by David Burch

Home Economists – Lorna Rhodes
and Linda Fraser

Line drawings by Lorraine Harrison

The publishers would like to thank the
following for kindly loaning equipment
for photography:

Reject China Shop
Bella Figura
J. K. Hill
The Bramley Hedge Shop

Note

All recipes serve four people unless
otherwise specified.

INTRODUCTION

Born in Suzhou;
Eat in Guangzhou;
Dress in Hangzhou;
Die in Liuzhou.
Old Chinese proverb

Guangzhou is the old city of Canton, for 800 years the center of contact between the East and West in the South China Seas. Thence came Western traders eager to buy Chinese silks and tea and from there left the early immigrants who settled in Singapore and California – called by the Cantonese The Gold Mountain. Others settled in Limehouse in London and opened the first Chinese eating houses in the UK, the ancestors of the modern Chinese restaurants.

Canton, the principal city of the province of Guangdong, is at the head of the Pearl River Estuary while the island of Hong Kong lies at the mouth of the same estuary. Guangdong is a rich farming land with paddy fields shining in the morning sun, waterways alive with ducks and lined with orchards of subtropical fruits. Everywhere there is growth and abundance. Northern Guangdong is ringed with mountains at whose feet lie orange groves and tea gardens, while the long coastline is dotted with bays and tiny coves where turtles come to lay their eggs, and shellfish and shrimp are plentiful. Farmers tend small plots of green vegetables which are ready for harvesting within two months of being sown, while others raise fish in great freshwater tanks.

In Guangdong live not only Cantonese-speaking people but also Hakka and Chaozhou people speaking their own forms of Chinese and having their own culture. Each group has contributed to the renown of Cantonese cooking. The Cantonese themselves cook their foods quickly using peanut oil to give it a characteristic flavor and including fresh vegetables in many of their dishes. They season their foods with soy, sesame, sugar, vinegar and chili peppers. Hakka people who live on the East river, steam many of their dishes. Their food is more oily, more slowly cooked and often more highly seasoned than the dishes of the Cantonese population. Chaozhou people live near the coast, and traditionally, many of them spend much of their lives with their families at sea, fishing. Fish, seafood, salted and preserved foods all play a large part in their cooking which is often sweeter and more highly decorated than other Southern peoples. They frequently use fruit as well as vegetables in a dish.

The cooking of a community mirrors the variety and quality of its produce, and in Guangdong there is a wealth of fresh foods available. The ducks and chickens and even the fish arrive live at the markets to be cooked at the peak of freshness. Small fishing boats in Hong Kong sell freshly caught live crabs, while other fishermen gather oysters from the beds in the shallow bays. Everywhere this food is transformed into miraculous dishes cooked in a moment, still full of their natural flavors, and seasoned to bring out their richness. Such is the background to Cantonese cooking.

It is quite possible to recreate many Cantonese dishes in our own kitchens in the West, since the sauces and flavorings are widely available in both Chinese and Western supermarkets. Judicious shopping for the very freshest vegetables and fish, fresh chickens and flavorful pork, although not necessarily the most expensive cuts, yields great returns.

Cantonese cooking methods

The basic method of Cantonese cooking is stir-frying. Foods for stir-frying are cut into thin slices or strips and cooked very quickly over high heat in a little oil so that the outside of the food is sealed while the inside remains moist. A Cantonese chef using a wok holds it over searing heat, raising or lowering the pan with one hand to control the temperature while keeping the food constantly on the move using a flat scoop in the other hand.

A true stir-fried dish has no gravy when it is finished and only a light final seasoning of soy, sugar or salt. It is dependent for its results on split-second timing, and should, therefore, be eaten immediately after it is cooked.

Bigger pieces of meat, including chicken pieces with bones, requiring longer cooking are stir-fried and then braised for a few minutes in a sauce to finish their cooking. Braised dishes do not require the split-second timing of a stir-fried dish and can wait for a few minutes before being served.

Often foods for Cantonese dishes are deep-fried either at the beginning of the cooking process or after they have already been cooked, as a final finishing stage. Not many Cantonese dishes are only deep-fried.

Steaming over boiling water is another very typical Cantonese form of cooking. Meats, fish, vegetables and soups can all be cooked in this way. The traditional southern Chinese kitchen does not have an oven, and a steamer takes its place for many cooking processes. Foods cooked in a steamer retain their shape and soups remain clear.

Equipment for Cantonese cooking

There is no need to buy any special equipment to cook Cantonese foods; ordinary Western pans and utensils can be used successfully for any cooking process. However many people are familiar with the curved-bottomed, wide-topped Chinese skillets, called woks, and enjoy using them. On Western gas stoves they produce excellent results, and are easy to use. A round-bottomed wok does not, however, have sufficient contact with the source of heat on an electric stove to produce the fierce heat required for a good stir-fry. Cooking a stir-fry at too low a temperature is often the cause of greasy foods and stale flavors. Nowadays it is possible to buy flat bottomed woks which work well on electric stoves.

The Chinese traditionally deep-fry in a wok with about 2½ cups of hot oil before pouring out all but a couple of tablespoons of the oil to continue cooking in the same pan. In a Western kitchen, however, it seems more practical to use a separate deep-fat oil pan with a fine mesh basket for the deep-frying and then to ladle a few spoons of the hot oil into a wok for the final stage of the cooking. Always heat the wok before adding the oil to prevent any food from sticking. Flat-bottomed woks should *never* be used for deep-frying because the ratio of volume of oil to depth of pan allows them to overflow when the foods are submerged in the hot oil.

Woks are also used in Chinese kitchens as the bases for the bamboo steaming baskets. These are circular bamboo boxes with lattice-work bottoms, each box fitting tightly onto the rim of another and the top box covered in a domed woven bamboo lid. A set is made up of two or three tiers and a lid; they are frequently sold in Western as well as Chinese stores. In these steamers it is possible to cook several dishes over one pan of boiling water. Foods are placed in bowls or plates in the baskets. It is, however, quite possible to substitute an ordinary Western steamer for a bamboo steamer, but often it is difficult to fit big bowls and plates into a Western steamer. If you are using a Chinese steamer and wok, it is better to hold the wok steady with a wire ring. Times for steaming dishes given in the recipes can only be approximate since individual stoves and steamers can vary greatly in the times required for a particular dish.

What to drink with a Cantonese meal

Beer goes well with almost all Chinese meals, or if you wish to drink wine, try a robust red wine such as a Cotes du Rhône or Corbières which will not get lost with Chinese food. Green flower-flavored teas, such as jasmine, can be drunk before or after a meal, but not with it or they will spoil the flavor of the food. If you want to drink tea with a Chinese meal, try a half-fermented tea such as Oolong or Gunpowder. *Puer,* a black tea from Yunnan is very popular in Hong Kong as an accompaniment for rich foods, since it is considered to be a good digestive. All these teas are available at Chinese supermarkets.

Serving quantities

Ordinary Cantonese meals are made up of several dishes each of equal importance. The number of people eating a meal will largely dictate the number of dishes. The serving numbers given above each recipe are a rough guide to the number each dish will feed when included in a meal for four people. All soups are for four people, and large birds and fish serving many people are, obviously, more suitable for a big dinner than a family meal.

GLOSSARY OF INGREDIENTS

Baby corn cobs: tiny corn cobs, sold canned or occasionally fresh.

Bamboo shoots: young shoots of bamboo. Sold canned in the West, once opened, they can be kept fresh by reboiling in fresh water every two to three days and should be stored in the refrigerator. *Salted bamboo shoots,* have a strong, sour flavor and can be kept for years. Sold in packages.

Bean curd: a fresh creamy curd made from soybeans. Sold in squares of varying weights. *Silken tofu* is unpressed bean curd sold in long-life packages, used mainly in soups.

Black beans: fermented soy or black beans with a strong salty flavor. Sold in bags.

Bitter melons: see Vegetable melons.

Black fungus: thin dried leaves of fungi with a delicate smoky flavor and a crunchy texture. Always soak before use. Sold in packages.

Board duck: a flat cream-colored dried duck with a smoky bacon flavor.

Bok choi: small cabbages with wide white stalks, joined together at the base, and dark green leaves, they look much like miniature Swiss chard. Sold in bunches.

Bottle squash: see Vegetable melons.

Chinese chives: the pointed flowering stalks and the narrow green leaves of Chinese chives are sold fresh. They have a strong garlicky flavor and a delicate texture.

Chinese kale: rather similar in form to *choi sam,* sometimes called Chinese broccoli, but with coarse, tough leaves and stalks and white flowers. Peel the stems before cooking. Sold in bunches.

Chinese lettuce: solid long lettuce that look a bit like romaine.

Chinese sausages: resemble thin salami.

Choi sam: the most delicate Chinese cabbage, has small, bright green leaves, green stalks and yellow flowers. Sold in bunches.

Cinnamon stick: smooth round sticks of rolled cinnamon bark, with a mild cinnamon flavor.

Crystal sugar: somewhat less sweet than refined Western sugar, it gives a syrupy consistency to sauces.

Dried orange peel: made from the skins of Chinese oranges, with a flavor similar to tangerines.

Dried mushrooms: they have a delicate flavor and a slightly chewy texture. Always soak before use.

Dried shrimp: These shrimp have a strong sea tang and will give a lift to any savory dish. Always soak before use.

11

Five-spice powder: a tangy mixed spice used in small quantities in savory dishes.

Fuzzy melons: see Vegetable melons.

Ginger: fresh rhizomes of the ginger plant are used extensively as a flavoring in Cantonese cooking. Buy firm shiny-skinned roots and use either peeled or unpeeled. Young ginger shoots are the fresh ginger sprouts, more delicate in taste and texture.

Glutinous rice: a round-grain white rice with a high gluten content, very sticky when cooked. Always soak before cooking.

Hoisin sauce: a Cantonese flavoring sauce made from soy beans, sugar and vinegar.

Kelp: long fronds of dried seaweed. When cooked it has an iodine flavor. Used for soup in Cantonese cooking.

Lotus leaves: the dried leaves of a water lily. Soak in boiling water before use. Sold in bunches.

Luffa: see Vegetable melons.

Maltose: a sugar syrup made from wheat starch. Substitute honey.

Noodles: wheat flour egg noodles for Cantonese cooking come in flat and round varieties. Use flat for soups and round for frying. Rice flour noodles include dried *rice vermicelli* and fresh soft noodles called *ho.* Use *ho* immediately after purchase; they do not keep well.

Oyster sauce: a Cantonese sauce used for flavoring vegetables and some meat dishes, it has a rich savory flavor which is not at all fishy.

Pickled cabbage or mustard greens: salted pickled cabbage with a sour flavor; rinse well before use. Sold usually in cans.

Potato flour: used as a thickening agent and less sticky than cornstarch.

Rice: long-grain rice is the standard southern Chinese rice. Use any variety of long-grain rice, and always wash well in several baths of cold water. Alternatively, use "converted" rice which requires no washing.

Rice wine: made from glutinous rice, it is a rather coarse weak spirit about 16° proof. Substitute dry sherry.

Sesame oil: a delicate-flavored oil extracted from sesame seeds. Do not overheat if using for frying since the flavor is destroyed by high temperatures.

Shrimp: raw shrimp are gray in color, fresh or frozen with their shells. Cooked shrimp are pink, with or without their shells and either frozen or fresh. Always remove the dark intestinal cord from the center of raw shrimp before use.

Sichuan peppercorns: a dried calex which looks much like a brown clove. The flavor is more spicy than hot.

Sichuan preserved vegetable: the peppery club stalk of another variety of Chinese cabbage preserved with hot spices. Rinse before use. Sold in cans, it will keep for months in the refrigerator in a covered clean container.

Snow peas: delicate flavored peas eaten whole with their pods.

Soy sauce: made from soybeans, adds color and flavor to all savory dishes. Sold frequently as *light soy sauce;* (labeled Superior Soy on Chinese mainland bottles) a lighter, saltier, soy sauce, while *dark soy sauce* (labeled Soy, superior sauce on Chinese mainland bottles) is a heavier, richer-flavored soy sauce.

Sour plums: the dried fruit of the Japanese apricot, with a sour flavor. Sold pickled in brine in jars.

Star anise: star-shaped dried calex and seeds with a strong anise flavor. Use in small quantities only.

Straw mushrooms: ball shaped mushrooms with a delicate woodland flavor. Sold canned.

Vegetable melons: the Chinese use a wide range of gourds or vegetable melons, among them are *bitter melons* which have a light green blistered skin and are about the size of small ridge cucumbers. Always blanch in boiling water to lessen the bitter flavor. A *bottle squash* has a bright green shiny skin and is shaped like a pointed vegetable marrow, with a delicate firm flesh. *Fuzzy melons* have a slightly duller green skin covered in fine hairs and are shaped like fat cucumbers, also with a delicate refreshing flavor. *Luffas* or silk gourds are shaped like a cucumber, dark green in color with marked ridges running along their length; these become more pronounced with age. They have a pleasing fresh flavor when young. *Winter melons* are large green-skinned gourds often weighing up to 8 lb. They have a delicate flavor and a marvellous melting texture.

Vinegar: Chinese vinegar made from rice lacks the astringency of malt vinegar. Both black and white varieties are sold in the West. *Red vinegar* is made from sorghum and has a spicy flavor.

Water chestnuts: crunchy round tubers. Sold mainly in cans in the West, they can be stored in a freezer after opening.

Water spinach: grown in swampy land, it has crunchy hollow stems and soft green leaves.

Winter melon: see Vegetable melons.

Wood ear mushrooms: a dried white almost transparent fungus which grows in the form of small cushions. Soak before use.

Wuntun skins: small squares of thin pasta. Bought fresh in packages from Chinese grocers. They do not keep well as skins, but once filled with *wuntun* filling, they can be deep-frozen.

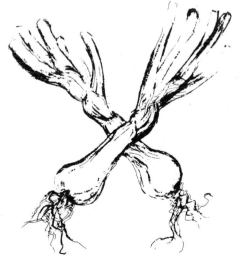

MEAT

For Cantonese cooks the word 'meat' implies pork, although beef, lamb and rabbit are used in Cantonese cooking. Pork is the most commonly eaten meat in family meals.

In China meat is cut off the bone in layers of muscle, rather than across the muscle and into roasts as is usual in the West. Western cuts of meat, such as boned loin or shoulder pork top round or thick flank steak, can, however, be made into excellent stir-fries. It is important to see that the meat, whatever cut is used, is free from fat, skin or gristle unless otherwise directed in the recipe. Tenderness in meat is an important quality for Chinese cooks, and to encourage this, pork and beef should always be cut into slices or shreds against the grain. Marinades in Cantonese cooking help tenderize meat and improve its flavor. A basic marinade for meat usually includes soy sauce, rice wine, sugar and cornstarch. Meat is usually fried at some stage in Cantonese cooking. Peanut oil or lard is used and fried at a much higher temperature than is usual in the West; this results in a lot of spluttering as the marinated meat hits the oil.

A Cantonese Meal for Four

Cantonese Roast Pork (page 16),
Cantonese Curried Chicken (page 34),
Stir-Fried Snow Peas (page 70),
Egg and Shrimp Fu Yung (page 60),
Chicken Giblet and Watercress Soup (page 77)
and *Plain Boiled Rice (page 80)*

Yuet Shi Cha Siu
Cantonese Roast Pork
Serves 2

This is one of the most famous Cantonese dishes, and in China is usually bought freshly cooked from a cooked meat shop. It is easy to make and delicious. Serve as a cold dish in a several-course meal, or use as an ingredient in other dishes.

10 oz. pork tenderloin in one piece
MARINADE:
¼ cup sugar
¼ cup hoisin sauce
2 tablespoons rice wine
2 tablespoons dark soy sauce
2 teaspoons salt

a pinch of five-spice powder
2 cloves garlic, crushed
GLAZE:
2 teaspoons sesame oil
2 teaspoons sugar
2 teaspoons red vinegar
a pinch of five-spice powder

Prepare the marinade first. Mix together the ingredients and use to marinate the pork for 6 hours, turning occasionally to make sure it is all well-coated.

Hang the pork tenderloin from the bars of the highest shelf in a moderately hot oven (375°F). Put a drip pan underneath the pork. Roast for 25 minutes until the pork is bright red, then paint it all over with the remaining marinade. Cook for an additional 25 minutes, checking that the meat does not begin to burn. If necessary, repaint with the marinade.

Meanwhile heat the glaze ingredients in a small saucepan over low heat until the sugar has dissolved.

When the pork is cooked and while it is still hot, paint it all over with the glaze. Leave to cool before slicing and serving.

Ku Lou Yuk
Sweet and Sour Pork

Serves 1

---

6 oz. boneless pork, cut into 1-inch cubes
oil for deep-frying
2 scallions, chopped
1 clove garlic, chopped
4 water chestnuts, thinly sliced
1¾ cups red or green pepper, seeded and cut
    into 1-inch pieces
½ cup canned pineapple chunks, drained

MARINADE:
2 teaspoons soy sauce
1 teaspoon rice wine
2 teaspoons cornstarch
SEASONING SAUCE:
1 tablespoon soy sauce
2 tablespoons sugar
2 tablespoons rice vinegar
⅓ cup water
a pinch of salt
2 teaspoons cornstarch
½ teaspoon sesame oil

Prepare the marinade first. Mix together the ingredients and use to marinate the pork for 30 minutes.

Meanwhile mix the seasoning sauce ingredients in a small bowl.

Deep-fry the pork in very hot oil for about 2 minutes before lifting out and draining well.

In a wok or large skillet heat 1 tablespoon oil and fry the onion and garlic for 30 seconds. Add the water chestnuts and pepper and stir-fry for 1 minute, then add the pork and pineapple. Continue stir-frying for another 30 seconds and pour in the seasoning sauce. Stir until it thickens, then serve.

Sam Shik Wat Yuk
Stir-fried Pork with Bamboo Shoots and Black Fungus

Serves 1

---

6 oz. lean boneless pork, cut into very thin
   slices about 1 inch square
3 pieces black fungus
oil for deep-frying
2 scallions cut into ½-inch lengths
1 teaspoon minced ginger root
1 clove garlic, minced
3 tablespoons bamboo shoots, sliced
3 tablespoons diced cucumber
1 teaspoon sesame oil
MARINADE:
1 tablespoon beaten egg

1 tablespoon soy sauce
1 teaspoon sesame oil
¼ teaspoon sichuan pepper, ground
a pinch of salt
a pinch of five-spice powder
1 tablespoon cornstarch
SEASONING SAUCE:
4 tablespoons stock
1 teaspoon rice wine
1 tablespoon light soy sauce
2 teaspoons rice vinegar
1 teaspoon cornstarch

Prepare the marinade first. Mix together the ingredients in a small bowl and use to marinate the pork slices for 1 hour.

Meanwhile soak the black fungus in warm water for 30 minutes. Rinse well and cut into strips, discarding any hard pieces.

Mix together the seasoning sauce ingredients in a small bowl.

Deep-fry the pork in very hot oil for 1½ minutes, then drain well.

In a wok or large skillet heat 2 tablespoons oil and stir-fry the onion, ginger root and garlic for 15 seconds. Add all the vegetables and continue stir-frying for another 30 seconds. Add the pork slices and stir-fry for a few moments before pouring in the seasoning sauce. Bring to a boil and serve sprinkled with the sesame oil.

Stir-Fried Pork with Bamboo Shoots and
Black Fungus

Ng Heung Zuk YukPei
Barbecued Spareribs

Serves 1 to 2

---

1 lb. spareribs, chopped into 1½-inch lengths
oil for deep-frying
3 scallions, cut into 2-inch lengths
3 slices ginger root, chopped
3 cloves garlic, crushed
salt
MARINADE:
2 tablespoons soy sauce
1 tablespoon cornstarch

SEASONING SAUCE:
2 tablespoons rice wine
2 tablespoons soy sauce
3 tablespoons sugar
2 tablespoons hoisin sauce
1 teaspoon salt
a pinch of five-spice powder

Prepare the marinade first. Mix together the ingredients and use to marinate the spareribs for 1 hour.

Meanwhile prepare the seasoning sauce by mixing all the ingredients together.

Deep-fry the spareribs in hot oil for 45 seconds, then lift out and drain well.

In a casserole or saucepan heat 2 tablespoons oil and stir-fry the onion, ginger root and garlic for 15 seconds. Pour in the seasoning sauce and bring to a boil. Add the spareribs and cover the pan. Reduce the heat and simmer for 1 hour. Towards the end of this time, check the seasoning, adding salt to taste if necessary, and watch to see the sauce does not burn at the bottom of the pan. Serve hot.

Sin Gu Sz Kua Yuk
Pork with Luffa and Mushrooms

Serves 1

6 oz. lean boneless pork, cut into small cubes
6 oz. luffa
oil for deep-frying
3 scallions cut into short lengths
¼ lb. (1½ cups) small button mushrooms,
    wiped and trimmed
salt and ground sichuan pepper to taste
½ teaspoon sesame oil

MARINADE:
2 teaspoons rice wine
1 teaspoon grated ginger root
1 teaspoon cornstarch
a pinch of salt
SEASONING SAUCE:
½ cup well-seasoned stock
1 tablespoon rice wine
THICKENING PASTE:
1 teaspoon cornstarch
2 teaspoons water

Prepare the marinade first. Mix together the ingredients and use to marinate the pork for 30 minutes.

Meanwhile prepare the luffa by paring off the ridged edges and cutting into 1-inch wedge-shaped pieces.

Mix the seasoning sauce in a small bowl. Mix the thickening paste in a small bowl.

Deep-fry the pork cubes in hot oil for 1½ minutes, then drain well.

In a wok or large skillet heat 2 tablespoons oil and stir-fry the onion for 15 seconds. Add the mushrooms, then the luffa and continue stir-frying for another 30 seconds. Mix in the pork cubes, then pour in the seasoning sauce. Cover the pan with a lid and simmer for about 5 minutes, until the luffa is soft. Thicken the sauce with the cornstarch paste, adjust the seasoning with salt and sichuan pepper to taste and serve sprinkled with sesame oil.

Beng Tung Zau Ji
Steamed Crystal Pork

Serves 6

It is most important in this dish to use Chinese crystal sugar, which gives the sauce a rich slippery texture without being overpoweringly sweet.

3 lb. picnic ham with bone. Deeply score the skin in a diamond pattern
1 tablespoon soy sauce
½ tablespoon rice wine
oil for deep-frying
10 oz. crystal sugar
3 tablespoons rice wine
1 teaspoon salt
½ teaspoon pepper

6 slices ginger root
½ lb. choi sam
1¼ cups well-seasoned chicken stock
salt and pepper
THICKENING PASTE:
½ tablespoon cornstarch mixed with
1 tablespoon water

Paint the ham all over with the soy sauce and rice wine.

Heat the oil for deep-frying and deep-fry the ham in one piece in the hot oil until it darkens in color, but do not allow the skin to blister. If possible use an electric deep-fryer for this because the meat splutters and spits when it hits the hot fat. Lift out and drain.

Place the ham with the sugar, rice wine, salt, pepper and ginger root in a bowl and steam it over fast-boiling water until the meat falls away from the bone, about 3½ hours.

Meanwhile cook the *choi sam* in boiling water for 2 minutes, then refresh in cold water.

When the meat is cooked, lift it from the bowl on to a heated platter, reserving the cooking juices. Boil the chicken stock and reheat the *choi sam* before draining and arranging around the meat.

Bring about ⅔ cup of the reserved juices to a boil in a small pan, season to taste with a little salt or pepper, thicken with the cornstarch and pour over the meat. Serve at once.

Note: The diners pick the meat from the roast with their chopsticks and can help themselves to a spoonful of the sauce with their soup spoons.

Choi Sam Chau Yuk
Pork with Ginger and Choi Sam

Serves 1

---

6 oz. lean boneless pork, *cut into small cubes*
oil *for deep-frying*
½ lb. choi sam, *washed and trimmed*
a pinch of salt
1 tablespoon sesame oil
2 slices ginger root, *minced*

2 teaspoons rice wine
salt and pepper
MARINADE:
1 teaspoon soy sauce
1 teaspoon rice wine
1 teaspoon cornstarch

Prepare the marinade first. Mix together the ingredients and use to marinate the pork for 30 minutes.

Deep-fry the pork in hot oil for 30 seconds. Lift out and drain well.

In a wok or large skillet heat 3 tablespoons oil and stir-fry the *choi sam* with a pinch of salt until it is soft, about 5 minutes. Lift out on to a heated platter and keep warm.

Heat the sesame oil in the same wok or skillet and stir-fry the ginger root for 15 seconds before adding the pork. Stir-fry for 30 seconds and then mix in the rice wine. Season with salt and pepper and spoon over the *choi sam* to serve.

Variation

You can substitute Western broccoli for *choi sam* . Cut the flowering heads into small pieces and peel the thick stalks before cutting them into strips about ¾ inch × 3 inches.

San Dung Chau Ngau Yuk
Stir-fried Beef with Winter Vegetables

Serves 1

This is a rather old-fashioned recipe from Hong Kong, in which the mildly sour flavor of preserved vegetables is a complete contrast to the more familiar flavor of fresh vegetables. The vegetables are called "winter" because they are preserved and so can be used when fresh vegetables are not available.

6 oz. lean boneless beef, cut into thin strips
4 dried mushrooms
1 oz. salted bamboo shoots
oil for deep-frying
1 clove garlic, chopped
2 slices ginger root
1 dried chili pepper, seeded and finely
   shredded
2 oz. pickled mustard greens, bought loose or
   canned. Rinse and cut into strips 2 inches
   long

white pepper to taste
½ teaspoon sesame oil
MARINADE:
1 teaspoon rice wine
1 teaspoon cornstarch
1 teaspoon sugar
1 teaspoon soy sauce

Prepare the marinade first. Mix together the ingredients in a small bowl and use to marinate the beef for 30 minutes.

Meanwhile prepare the dried vegetables. Soak the dried mushrooms in hot water for 30 minutes, then discard the hard stalks and slice the caps. Rinse the salted bamboo shoots and drop them into a pan of boiling water. Boil for 1 minute, then drain and rinse in cold water. Return to a pan of freshly boiling water and boil again for 1 minute before draining and rinsing. This process is to reduce the strong, sour flavor of salted bamboo; if necessary repeat the process another time. Finally cut into 2-inch lengths.

Deep-fry the beef for 30 seconds in hot oil, then drain well.

In a wok or large skillet heat 2 tablespoons oil and stir-fry the garlic, ginger root and chili pepper over moderate heat for 15 seconds. Add the bamboo shoots, mushrooms and mustard greens and continue to stir-fry for another minute. Add the beef and a splash of water and cook for 30 seconds over high heat. Season with white pepper and serve sprinkled with sesame oil.

Gu Lou Ngau Yuk Un
Beef Meat Balls in a Sweet and Sour Sauce
Makes 4 meat balls

6 oz. lean boneless beef, cut into small pieces
cornstarch for dusting
oil for deep-frying
1 tablespoon minced scallions
SEASONING FOR MEAT BALLS:
2 tablespoons rice wine
1 teaspoon grated ginger root
1 teaspoon minced scallions
1 teaspoon soy sauce
1/4 teaspoon sesame oil

2 teaspoons egg white
1/2 teaspoon salt
a pinch of freshly ground black pepper
SWEET AND SOUR SAUCE:
1 tablespoon soy sauce
2 tablespoons sugar
2 tablespoons rice vinegar
1/4 cup water
1/2 tablespoon cornstarch
1/2 teaspoon sesame oil
a pinch of salt

First make the meat balls. Pile the meat in the center of a strong chopping board and pound it with the blunt edge of a meat cleaver. Work from one side to the other across the board, hardly lifting the blade from the meat. Use the flat of the blade to fold the meat back on top of itself, and pound across the meat again at right angles to the previous movement. Continue the pounding and folding until the meat becomes a homogeneous mass. Occasionally sprinkle it with the rice wine.

When the meat is reduced to a smooth pulp, transfer it to a bowl and blend in the remaining seasoning ingredients. Beat very thoroughly before dividing the mixture into four pieces.

Wet your hands to prevent the paste sticking to them and roll each portion into a ball between your palms. Dust with the dry cornstarch.

Mix the sweet and sour sauce ingredients in a small bowl. Deep-fry the meat balls in hot oil for 2 minutes and then drain well.

In a wok or large skillet heat 1 tablespoon oil and pour in the seasoning sauce. Bring to a boil stirring continuously and slide in the meat balls. See they are well-coated in the sauce and serve garnished with minced scallions.

Ngau Yuk Chau Bok Choi
Fried Beef with Bok Choi

Serves 1

---

6 oz. lean beef, cut into matchstick shreds
½ lb. bok choi
oil for deep-frying
1 tablespoon soy sauce

MARINADE:
1 teaspoon soy sauce
1 teaspoon rice wine
1 teaspoon grated ginger root
½ teaspoon sugar
½ teaspoon cornstarch

Prepare the marinade first. Mix together the ingredients in a small bowl and use to marinate the shredded beef for 45 minutes.

Wash the *bok choi* and separate the individual leaves. Cut them into 3-inch lengths.

Deep-fry the beef in hot oil for 30 seconds, then drain well.

In a wok or large skillet heat 2 tablespoons oil and stir-fry the *bok choi* for about 2 minutes until it is just cooked but still crisp. Stir in the meat and mix well with the *bok choi*. Season with the soy sauce and serve immediately.

Ho You Ngau Yuk
Beef with Oyster Sauce

Serves 1

---

6 oz. lean boneless beef, cut into thin slices
oil for deep-frying
1 scallion, cut into 2-inch lengths
2 slices ginger root
½ teaspoon sugar
1 tablespoon oyster sauce

MARINADE:
1 teaspoon light soy sauce
1 teaspoon beaten egg
¼ teaspoon sugar
1 teaspoon cornstarch
a pinch of salt and pepper

Prepare the marinade first. Mix together the ingredients in a small bowl and use to marinate the beef slices for 30 minutes.

Deep-fry the beef in hot oil for 30 seconds. Lift out and drain well.

In a wok or large skillet heat 2 tablespoons oil and stir-fry the onion and ginger for 15 seconds. Add the beef, sprinkle it with the sugar and stir-fry for 20 seconds before stirring in the oyster sauce. Serve at once.

Fried Beef with Bok Choi

BIRDS

Cantonese cooks have a wide range of birds in their repertoire, ranging from battery raised chickens to rice birds, pheasants and even sea-hawks. Chickens and ducks are used almost equally, often being interchangeable in a recipe. In the markets of Hong Kong, it is customary to buy a live bird and then either to have it killed and plucked at the stall or to take it home to fatten for a few days before being eaten.

Small dishes of duck or chicken often use only breast meat, but leg and wing meat can be stir-fried – or braised equally well. Meat for these dishes must always be cut with the grain to insure it does not toughen in cooking. Birds cooked whole are usually chopped into pieces before being served. The legs and wings are removed and the bird is cut in half through the rib cage separating the breast from the backbone. The backbone is discarded and the breast chopped first lengthwise in half and then into 1-inch pieces. The legs and wings are chopped into similar-sized pieces and the bird is reassembled on a heated platter.

Se Sik Za Gai
Four-colored Chicken

Serves 2

6 oz. boneless chicken breast, cut into thin slices
oil for deep-frying
2 tablespoons chicken fat or use oil
2 slices ginger root
1 cup fresh broccoli florets
2 oz. canned baby corn cobs, cut in half lengthwise
2 oz. lean cooked ham cut into thin pieces 1 inch × 1½ inches
⅓ cup well-seasoned chicken stock

salt and pepper
½ teaspoon sesame oil
MARINADE:
1 teaspoon rice wine
1 scallion, minced
½ teaspoon grated ginger root
2 teaspoons egg white
1 teaspoon cornstarch
a pinch of salt
THICKENING PASTE:
1 teaspoon cornstarch mixed with
2 teaspoons water

Prepare the marinade first. Mix together the ingredients in a small bowl and use to marinate the chicken slices for 30 minutes.

Deep-fry the chicken in hot oil over high heat for 30 seconds, then lift out and drain well.

In a wok or large skillet heat the chicken fat and stir-fry the ginger root for 15 seconds before adding the broccoli, corn cobs and ham. Stir-fry for 30 seconds, then mix in the chicken and continue to stir-fry for another 30 seconds. Pour in the stock and bring to a boil. Season to taste and thicken with the cornstarch paste. Sprinkle with the sesame oil and serve hot.

Tung Ji Shi Yao Gai
Chicken in Soy Sauce

Serves 4

2½ lb roasting chicken
10 shallots or small onions
3 slices ginger root
salt and pepper

SEASONING SAUCE:
2 tablespoons crystal sugar
6 tablespoons dark soy sauce
5 tablespoons light soy sauce
1¼ cups water

Put all the ingredients for the seasoning sauce into a large casserole and bring them to a boil. Add the chicken, onion, and ginger root. If the chicken is not completely covered by the seasoning sauce, add sufficient water to cover. Return to a boil, skim the top of the stock for about 5 minutes and then reduce the heat and cover the pan. Simmer until the chicken is cooked, about 2 hours, turning the chicken occasionally in the stock during the cooking. Season to taste and serve on a heated platter, chopped into pieces.

Ma Lat Shau Sz Gai
Sesame and Chili Hand-torn Chicken

Serves 1

1 chicken leg, ¾ lb. (approx.)
a pinch of salt
2 whole scallions, trimmed
2 tablespoons sesame oil

1 teaspoon sugar
4 dried chili peppers cut into shreds
3 scallions, very finely minced

Put the chicken leg, salt and 2 scallions into a bowl and steam them over fast-boiling water for 30 minutes.

When the chicken is cooked, tear the meat from the bones into strips. Strain and reserve the cooking juices. Place the chicken strips in a serving bowl.

Heat the sesame oil in a small pan. Add the sugar and chili peppers and cook gently until the sugar has dissolved. Pour in the reserved cooking juices and mix well before pouring over the chicken. Leave to marinate for at least 4 hours in the refrigerator. Mix in the minced scallions and serve.

Sesame and Chili Hand-torn Chicken

Gam Bai Za Kai Zai
Crispy Fried Chicken
Serves 2

1 lb. rock Cornish hen or *very small chicken*
1 teaspoon five-spice powder
1 teaspoon salt
2 teaspoons rice vinegar
2 teaspoons clear honey
oil for deep-frying

DIPPING SAUCE (see page 37):
1 tablespoon ground sichuan peppercorns
1 tablespoon salt

Rub the chicken all over with a mixture of the five-spice powder and salt, and hang it in a cold place for at least 4 hours.

Meanwhile mix the vinegar and honey over low heat to make a syrup and leave to cool.

Paint the chicken all over with the syrup and leave for a few moments, before repainting to make sure it is completely coated.

Hang the chicken in a moving current of air for about 3 hours until the skin is dry and leathery. Outside on a good dry day is ideal, but failing this, use an electric fan or heater running at cold. The chicken does not need heat to dry, only moving air.

Heat the oil in a large pan or an electric deep-fryer and very carefully lower in the chicken. Immediately reduce the heat and deep-fry for 10 minutes. Lift out the chicken and drain for a few minutes while the oil is reheating. When it is very hot, return the chicken for an additional 2 minutes to crisp the skin. Take care it does not burn at this stage. Chop into bite-sized pieces and serve at once with the pepper-salt dip.

Sai Ning Zin Yun Gai
Lemon Chicken

6 chicken wings, each chopped into 4 pieces
oil for deep-frying
2 scallions cut into ½-inch lengths
3 slices ginger root
MARINADE:
1 teaspoon dark soy sauce
1 teaspoon rice wine
a pinch of salt
1 teaspoon cornstarch

SEASONING SAUCE:
1 tablespoon black vinegar
1½ tablespoons sugar
1 tablespoon soy sauce
½ lemon cut into 8 pieces
¼ cup water
THICKENING PASTE:
½ tablespoon cornstarch mixed with
1 tablespoon water

Prepare the marinade first. Mix together the ingredients and use to marinate the chicken wings for 30 minutes.

Meanwhile mix together the seasoning sauce ingredients in one small bowl and the thickening paste in another.

Deep-fry the chicken in hot oil for about 1 minute. Lift out and drain.

In a casserole or saucepan heat 2 tablespoons oil and stir-fry the scallions and ginger root for 15 seconds. Pour in the prepared seasoning sauce and bring to a boil. Add the chicken, cover the pan and leave to cook over low heat for 20 minutes. Check the seasoning and thicken the sauce before serving on a heated plate.

Guang Shi Ka Lei Gai
Cantonese Curried Chicken
Serves 2

Cantonese cooks are very willing to adapt popular foreign dishes to a Chinese style. Although curry is not a Chinese spice, curries such as this are very popular.

¾ lb. boneless, skinless chicken cut into
*   1½-inch pieces*
3 tablespoons oil
¼ cup thinly sliced onion
3 slices ginger root, minced
1 dried chili pepper (optional), seeded and
*   shredded*
1 teaspoon curry powder
a pinch of five-spice powder
¼ cup canned coconut milk (optional)

salt and pepper
SEASONING SAUCE:
3 fl. oz. chicken stock
2 teaspoons rice wine
1 teaspoon sugar
2 teaspoons light soy sauce
THICKENING PASTE:
1 teaspoon cornstarch mixed with
2 teaspoons water

In a wok or large skillet heat 3 tablespoons oil and stir-fry the chicken pieces until they are lightly browned all over. Lift out and set aside. If necessary add another tablespoon or so of oil to the pan and stir-fry the onion over low heat until it is transparent. Add the ginger root and chili pepper and continue stir-frying for another 30 seconds before adding the curry and five-spice powders. Stir briskly over high heat until the curry powder no longer smells raw, then add the chicken. Mix well with the curry before pouring in the seasoning sauce.

Cover the pan and simmer for 10 minutes, then remove the lid and stir in the coconut milk. Bring to a boil, stirring continuously, adjust the seasoning and thicken with the cornstarch paste. Serve hot.

Note: If not using coconut milk, increase the chicken stock to ⅔ cup and simmer for 15 minutes. Finish as above.

Guang Shi Ming Lou Cha Ngo
Cantonese Roast Goose

Serves 8

One of the most familiar sights in Hong Kong and the Chinatowns in the West are the shiny golden-brown geese and ducks in the windows of cooked meat shops.

1 small goose, 8 lb. (approx.)
SEASONING SPICES:
2 inches ginger root, chopped
2 teaspoons sichuan peppercorns
2 petals star anise
2-inch square dried orange peel or use thinly
   pared, fresh orange peel
4 teaspoons salt

GLAZE:
¼ cup water
2 teaspoons maltose or clear honey
DIPPING SAUCE (see page 37):
1 tablespoon salt
1 tablespoon ground sichuan peppercorns

Mix together the seasoning spices and put them inside the goose. Sew up the vent very securely. Pour a kettle of boiling water over the goose to tighten up the skin, then dry it carefully.

Make the glaze by mixing the ingredients in a small pan over moderate heat stirring continuously until the maltose is dissolved in the water. Paint the skin of the goose all over with this thin syrup and hang it up to dry in a moving current of air. Outside on a good dry day is ideal, for the goose does not need heat only wind, or use an electric fan or heater turned to cold. After 2 hours, repaint the goose and hang it to dry again for another 4 hours. When it is finished the skin should feel stiff and leathery.

Hang the goose from the top shelf of a hot oven (400°F). Put a drip pan underneath. Roast for 20 minutes, then reduce the heat to 375°F and continue cooking for another 1½ hours to 2 hours, depending on the size of the goose. Allow 15 minutes per pound and 15 minutes extra. It may be necessary to hang the goose the other way up halfway through the cooking.

Serve with the dipping sauce, either hot, carved in thin slices on a heated plate, or cold, chopped into small pieces as a course in a dinner.

Variations

This recipe can also be used for roasting a duck. Halve the quantity of spices and glaze used and cook for between 1 hour and 1½ hours, allowing 15 minutes per pound, plus 15 minutes extra.

Sai Yeung Choi Tun Fung Wong Ya
Board Duck, Chicken and Watercress Pot

Serves 6 to 8

½ board duck, 1 lb. (approx.)
½ chicken, 1½ lb. (approx.), chopped into
  3-inch pieces
1 lb. watercress, about 4 bunches, rinsed and
  picked over

2 slices ginger root
salt
light soy sauce

Rinse the duck well in cold water, then cook in boiling water for 15 minutes. Soak in cold water for another 10 minutes to rinse off the fat. Finally, chop it into 3-inch pieces.

Blanch the chicken pieces in boiling water for 5 minutes, then rinse in cold water.

Assemble the duck, chicken, watercress and ginger root in a casserole and cover completely with boiling water. Put the casserole into a steamer over boiling water and steam for 3 hours. Alternatively, place the casserole in a roasting pan half-filled with boiling water and cover completely with either the roasting pan lid or aluminum foil. Cook in a moderately slow oven (325°F) for 3 hours. Season to taste with salt and light soy sauce before serving.

Variation
5-6 slices smoked bacon can be substituted for the board duck if necessary.

Shun Dak Tsui Pei Ya
Shun Dak Duck

Serves 2

1½ lb. duck breast with bones
oil for deep-frying
SEASONING SAUCE:
8 sichuan peppercorns
2 petals star anise
1-inch cinnamon stick
8 cloves
2-inch square dried orange peel, or *use thinly
  pared, fresh orange peel*
1 teaspoon fennel seeds
¼ teaspoon licorice powder or *use fennel
  seeds*
3 tablespoons soy sauce

3 tablespoons rice wine
3 tablespoons crystal sugar
2 cups water
½ teaspoon salt
GLAZING SYRUP:
¼ cup vinegar
2 teaspoons maltose or *honey*
DIPPING SAUCE (see page 37):
1 tablespoon ground sichuan peppercorns
1 tablespoon salt
GARNISH:
deep-fried shrimp chips (optional)

First prepare the seasoning sauce. Tie the dry ingredients in a small clean piece of cheesecloth and put them with the soy sauce, rice wine, sugar, water and salt into a medium-sized saucepan. Bring to a boil and simmer for 20 minutes.

Meanwhile prepare the glaze by mixing the vinegar and maltose in a small saucepan over low heat until they are well-blended. Leave to cool.

Add the duck to the prepared seasoning sauce, cover the pan and cook over gentle heat for about 15 minutes. Turn the duck over to make sure it is all well-soaked in the spiced stock and cook for another 20 minutes.

Lift out the duck and leave to cool for a few moments before patting it dry and painting it all over with the glaze. Leave it on a rack in an airy place to cool and dry, about 3 hours.

During this time prepare the pepper-salt dip by mixing the salt and pepper in a dry pan and cooking them over low heat, until they smell fragrant. Shake the pan occasionally during the cooking, and store in a dry place until required.

When the duck is really dry, deep-fry the duck in hot oil until the skin is crisp, about 4 minutes. Lift out, drain quickly and chop into small pieces. Serve hot, garnished with deep-fried shrimp chips and with the pepper-salt dip on the side.

Zi Lo Chau Ya Bin
Duck with Pineapple and Ginger
Serves 1

This recipe is a Chaozhou dish, very dependent on fruit for its flavor.

6 oz. boneless, skinless duck, cut into thin
    shreds
oil for deep-frying
2-inch piece young ginger root
    cut into paper-thin slices
3 scallions cut into ½-inch lengths
1 pineapple ring, cut into 1-inch cubes
salt and pepper
1 teaspoon sesame oil

MARINADE:
½ teaspoon cornstarch
½ teaspoon sugar
½ teaspoon sesame oil
1 teaspoon rice wine
1 teaspoon soy sauce
a pinch of salt and pepper
SEASONING SAUCE:
1 tablespoon soy sauce
2 tablespoons sugar
2 tablespoons rice vinegar
3 tablespoons water
2 teaspoons cornstarch

Prepare the marinade first. Mix together the ingredients in a small bowl and use to marinate the duck shreds for 30 minutes.

Meanwhile mix together the seasoning sauce ingredients. Deep-fry the duck in very hot oil for 30 seconds. Lift out and drain.

In a wok or large skillet heat 2 tablespoons oil and stir-fry the ginger root and scallions for 30 seconds. Add the duck shreds and pineapple and continue to stir-fry for another 15 seconds before pouring in the seasoning sauce. Mix well and bring to a boil. Season to taste with salt and pepper and serve sprinkled with sesame oil.

Duck with Pineapple and Ginger

FISH & SHELLFISH

Choosing fish suitable for Chinese cooking poses some problems to the Western cook. The fish found in the South China Seas are very different from those in the Atlantic and Pacific Oceans, even though some may belong to the same species. It is, therefore, always necessary to substitute and compromise. In this chapter the fish I have suggested are good to eat, of roughly the same type as the original, and, since many Chinese fish dishes use a whole fish, look right on the plate. Always choose fresh-looking fish; a fresh baby haddock will give a better result than a tired carp in any dish.

Raw shrimp are the gray-colored ones sold in their shells. Always remove the dark digestive cord running through the center of their bodies before cooking. Pink prawns, sold either fresh or frozen, with or without their shells, have already been boiled and their flesh is too dry to cook successfully in many Chinese dishes.

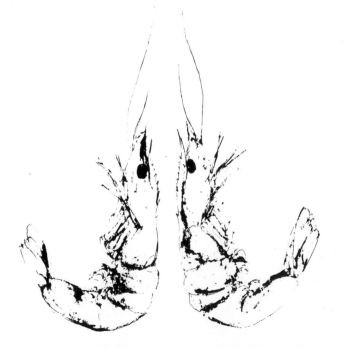

Keung Tsung Chau Yu
Sea Bass with Ginger and Onions
Serves 2

1 lb. sea bass, scaled, gutted and patted dry
3 tablespoons oil
1 inch ginger root, bruised
½ cup scallions, cut into 2-inch lengths
1 clove garlic, crushed
1 inch-square dried orange peel, or *use finely pared, fresh orange peel (Soften the dried orange peel in warm water before slicing finely)*
salt and pepper
½ teaspoon sesame oil
black pepper

SEASONING SAUCE:
1½ tablespoons rice wine
1¼ cups rich stock
½ teaspoon salt
2 teaspoons oyster sauce
1 tablespoon dark soy sauce
THICKENING PASTE:
2 teaspoons cornstarch mixed with
1 tablespoon water

First mix together the seasoning sauce ingredients in a small bowl.

Heat a wok or large skillet over moderate heat and add the oil. Fry the fish on both sides until the skin is lightly browned then lift it out carefully and set aside. Place the ginger root, scallions, garlic and orange shreds into the oil and stir-fry for about 15 seconds until they smell fragrant, then pour in the seasoning sauce.

Return the fish to the pan, cover and cook gently until the fish is done (when its eyes puff out), about 15 minutes. Lift the fish out on to a heated platter. Remove the ginger root from the stock and thicken with the cornstarch paste. Season to taste with salt and pepper and pour the finished sauce over the fish. Sprinkle with sesame oil and black pepper and serve hot.

Shun Dak Ching Lei Yu
Shun Dak Carp

Serves 6

1½ lb. mirror carp, scaled and gutted with
   the head and tail left on
1 teaspoon salt
cornstarch for dusting
6 scallions, cut into hair-fine threads
3 tablespoons ginger root cut into fine threads
STUFFING:
3 dried mushrooms
5 oz. lean ground pork

4 fresh shrimp, shelled, deveined and chopped
½ teaspoon salt
2 teaspoons sesame oil
1 teaspoon cornstarch
2 teaspoons rice wine
a pinch of pepper
SEASONING SAUCE:
2 tablespoons sesame oil
2 tablespoons soy sauce

First prepare the stuffing by soaking the mushrooms in hot water for 30 minutes, then discarding the hard stalks and chopping the caps finely. Blend all the ingredients for the stuffing together very thoroughly.

Pat the fish dry and sprinkle the skin with salt before dusting it inside and out with the cornstarch. Fill the stomach cavity with the prepared stuffing folding the thin flaps of skin over to close. Place the fish carefully on to a plate and put into a steamer over fast-boiling water. Steam for 30–40 minutes, until the eyes puff up and the fish is cooked.

Slide the fish carefully on to a heated platter and sprinkle it with the ginger root and scallion threads.

Heat the sesame oil and soy sauce in a small saucepan. When it comes to a boil, pour quickly over the ginger root and scallions and serve at once.

Shun Dak Carp

Gong Nam Chau Yu
Fried Fish

Serves 1

½ lb. fresh trout
cornstarch for rolling
oil for deep-frying
1 tablespoon black rice vinegar
salt and pepper
SAUCE:
2 dried mushrooms
2 tablespoons oil
2 scallions, cut into 1-inch lengths

1 thin slice lean pork
2½ tablespoons thinly sliced bamboo shoots
1½ tablespoons rice wine
1½ tablespoons soy sauce
1 tablespoon sugar
1 cup rich meat stock
THICKENING PASTE:
2 teaspoons cornstarch mixed with
2 teaspoons water

Prepare the sauce first. Soak the dried mushrooms in hot water for 30 minutes, then discard the hard stalks and cut the caps into thin slices.

In a wok or large skillet heat the oil and stir-fry the scallions for 15 seconds before adding the pork. Stir-fry for 30 seconds and then add the mushrooms and bamboo shoots. Stir-fry for another 30 seconds and season with the rice wine, soy sauce and sugar. Pour in the stock and bring to a boil. Set the sauce aside, keeping it warm.

Mix the thickening paste in a small bowl.

Roll the fish in the cornstarch, both inside and out. Heat the oil and deep-fry the fish in moderately hot oil for about 10 minutes, until the outside is crisp.

Reboil the sauce, thicken with the cornstarch paste and add the vinegar. Check the seasoning, adding salt and pepper if necessary. The moment the fish is lifted on to the heated platter pour the sauce over it – it should sizzle as the sauce touches the crisp fish skin. Serve at once.

Fan Ke Gu Lou Yu
Sweet and Sour Fish

Serves 2

---

1 rockfish about 1– 1½ lb. Leave on the head and tail, gut and score both sides several times
5 dried mushrooms
cornstarch for rolling
oil for deep-frying
2 scallions, cut into ½-inch lengths
3 slices ginger root
1 dried chili pepper, seeded and cut into shreds
MARINADE:
1 scallion, minced
1 teaspoon grated ginger root
1 teaspoon salt
2 tablespoons rice wine
SEASONING SAUCE:
1 tablespoon tomato paste
⅓ cup sugar
1 tablespoon cornstarch
1 teaspoon salt
⅓ cup white rice vinegar
⅓ cup water
1 teaspoon sesame oil

Prepare the marinade first. Mix together the ingredients in a wide bowl and marinate the fish for 30 minutes, turning frequently to make sure it is well-coated in the marinade.

Meanwhile soak the dried mushrooms in hot water for 30 minutes before discarding the hard stalks and slicing the caps.

Prepare the seasoning sauce in a small bowl and set aside.

Heat the oil for deep-frying, if possible in an electric fryer. Roll the fish in the cornstarch, then deep-fry it until it is cooked, about 5 minutes. The eyes will puff out when it is done. Drain well and keep warm on a platter.

In a wok or large skillet heat 1 tablespoon oil and stir-fry the scallions, ginger root, mushrooms and chili pepper for 30 seconds. Pour in the seasoning sauce and bring to a boil stirring continuously while it thickens. Spoon over the fish and serve.

Fo Tui Wui Long Ha
Braised Shrimp with Bamboo Shoots and Ham

Serves 2

½ lb raw shrimp, shelled and de-veined
oil for deep frying
2 scallions, cut into ½ inch lengths
2 slices ginger root
½ lb lean ham, cut into thin slices about
   1 inch × 2 inches
1¼ cups bamboo shoots, cut into similar sized
   slices
salt and pepper

MARINADE:
½ egg white
4 teaspoons rice wine
4 teaspoons cornstarch
½ teaspoon salt
SEASONING SAUCE:
1¼ cups stock, well-seasoned
1 tablespoon soy sauce
1 tablespoon rice wine
1 tablespoon cornstarch

Prepare the marinade first. Mix together the ingredients in a small bowl and marinate the shrimp for 30 minutes.

Meanwhile mix the seasoning sauce ingredients in another small bowl.

Deep-fry the shrimp in hot oil for 30 seconds, then lift out and drain.

In a wok or large skillet heat 2 tablespoons of oil and stir-fry the scallion and ginger root for 15 seconds. Add the ham and bamboo shoots and stir-fry for another 30 seconds before adding the shrimp. Pour in seasoning sauce and bring to a boil. Season with salt and pepper and serve.

Sun Bao Long Ha
Fried Shrimp

Serves 1

6 oz. raw shrimp in the shell, deveined or
   pink shrimp
oil for deep-frying
2 cloves garlic
1 teaspoon salt

MARINADE:
2 teaspoons grated ginger root
1½ tablespoons rice wine

Prepare the marinade first. Mix the grated ginger root and rice wine in a small bowl and marinate the shrimp for 30 minutes.

Pat the shrimp dry and deep-fry in hot oil for 1 minute. Drain well.

Just before you wish to eat, place the shrimp in a dry skillet with the garlic and salt and stir-fry over low heat until they are heated through.

Fried Shrimp

Sin Chong Nong Hai
Steamed Crabs

Serves 4

---

4 small crabs
oil for painting
1 tablespoon grated ginger root
1 teaspoon sesame oil
FISH PASTE:
1 tablespoon finely diced salt pork
3 oz. boneless, skinless white fish

2 teaspoons egg white
½ teaspoon rice wine
2 teaspoons cornstarch
SAUCE:
⅓ cup well-seasoned clear chicken stock
1 teaspoon cornstarch
salt and pepper

Clean the crabs by removing the legs and claws and lifting up the carapace (upper shell). Remove the stomach and feathery gills and discard. Scrape all the meat from the shell into a bowl. Crack the claws and legs, extract the meat, and add it to the bowl. Pick off any white meat from the carapace. Wash the empty shells very carefully, if necessary scrub them with a small brush, taking care not to crack them. Dry them carefully and brush inside of each with a little oil.

Make the fish paste according to the method given for meat balls on page 25. Blend the fish paste with the crabmeat and the grated ginger root. Fill each crab shell with the mixture, and smooth over the tops with the dampened back of a spoon.

Steam the stuffed crabs over fast-boiling water for 20 to 25 minutes, depending on the size of the crabs.

Meanwhile make the sauce by mixing the stock and cornstarch together in a small pan. Bring to a boil, season to taste with salt and pepper and leave at the side of the stove.

When the crabs are cooked, arrange them on a heated platter, spoon on the sauce and serve sprinkled with sesame oil.

BEANCURD & EGGS

China is a poor country, and for generations meat has been a luxury for most people, eaten only on special occasions. The everyday protein has commonly been bean curd, called *dau fu* in Cantonese, but often known as *tofu* in the West after the Japanese form of its name. *Tofu* is made from soybeans and is very rich in vegetable protein. The cream-colored squares look like an anemic custard, but the versatility of bean curd as an ingredient for cooking is unsurpassable – Chinese bean curd recipes run into many hundreds. It has a light pleasing taste which blends in well with other flavors.

Eggs are also a protein food for the Chinese. In the south, duck eggs are more popular than chicken eggs, while quail eggs are used whole and valued for their size. Raw duck eggs are preserved in salt, giving them a slight tangy flavor, which is much admired. Do not confuse these salted eggs, with their black soot coating, with the "100-year-old" duck eggs which are preserved in lime and ashes. "100-year-old" eggs are cut into pieces and eaten with a dip and are not generally used for cooking.

Ga Sheung Zu Dau Fu Un
Bean Curd Balls

Makes 14

---

10 oz. bean curd pressed between two plates
   for 4 hours
3 dried mushrooms
3 tablespoons minced carrots
2 tablespoons fava beans, skinned
1 teaspoon sesame oil
2 tablespoons potato flour

salt and pepper
flour for rolling
oil for deep-frying
DIPPING SAUCE (see page 37):
1 tablespoon salt
1 tablespoon ground sichuan peppercorns

Soak the dried mushrooms in hot water for 30 minutes, then discard the hard stalks and chop the caps very finely. Blend the bean curd, mushrooms, carrots and fava beans together with the sesame oil and potato flour into a very smooth paste. It is best to use a food processor for this, or beat the mixture against the sides of the bowl until it is quite smooth.

Dust your hands with flour and roll the paste into small walnut-sized balls.

Deep-fry the balls in moderately hot oil until they are golden-brown, about 1½ minutes. Drain on paper towels and serve hot with the dip on the side.

Bean Curd Balls

Ha Heung Jeong Dau Fu
Stuffed Bean Curd

Serves 2

¾ lb. bean curd, cut into 4 equal squares
1 tablespoon oil
1 teaspoon minced scallions
½ teaspoon grated ginger root
1 tablespoon oyster sauce
1 tablespoon light soy sauce
STUFFING:
2 oz. lean pork, pounded into a paste, for method see page 25

2 oz. raw shrimp, shelled and deveined and pounded into a paste, for method see page 25
1 scallion, very finely minced
¼ teaspoon rice wine
½ teaspoon light soy sauce
½ teaspoon salt
a pinch of pepper

Hollow out a small hole about 1 inch wide × ¾ inch deep in the center of each square of bean curd.

Make the stuffing by mixing the pork paste, shrimp paste and scraps of bean curd together in a bowl. Blend very thoroughly with the remaining stuffing ingredients until the mixture is a smooth paste; it is easier to do this in a food processor with a plastic blade attachment.

Fill the hollows in the bean curd squares with the prepared stuffing, smoothing the tops with the back of a dampened spoon. Arrange the bean curd squares on a small plate.

In a small saucepan heat the oil and gently stir-fry the scallion and ginger root for 15 seconds before stirring in the oyster and soy sauces together with 1 tablespoon water. Simmer for 3 minutes, then spoon this sauce over the bean curd.

Place the plate with the bean curd into a steamer over fast-boiling water and steam for 25 minutes. Serve hot.

Ma Ziu Heung Dau Fu
Bean Curd with Cucumber and Cashew Nuts

Serves 1

½ cup cashew nuts
oil for deep-frying
6 oz. bean curd pressed between two plates
   for 1 hour and then cut into 1-inch cubes
3 tablespoons sesame oil
2 cloves garlic, chopped
2 scallions, cut into 1-inch lengths
½ cucumber cut into 1-inch cubes
salt

SEASONING SAUCE:
2 tablespoons light soy sauce
2 tablespoons sugar
2 tablespoons red vinegar
2 tablespoons water
¼ teaspoon chili oil
THICKENING PASTE:
1 teaspoon cornstarch mixed with
2 teaspoons water

Heat the oil for deep-frying and deep-fry the cashew nuts over low heat until they turn golden-brown, about 4 minutes. Lift out and drain.

Reheat the oil and deep-fry the bean curd cubes for 2 minutes, until they also are golden colored. Drain well.

Mix the thickening paste in a small bowl.

In a wok or large skillet heat the sesame oil and stir-fry the garlic and scallions over moderate heat for 15 seconds. Add the cucumber and continue stir-frying for another minute before pouring in the seasoning sauce. Bring to a boil and thicken with the cornstarch paste. Finally quickly mix in the fried bean curd and cashew nuts, add salt to taste and serve at once.

Dung Gu Dau Fu Bao
Cantonese Bean Curd Pot
Serves 2

In the winter in Canton, people like to ward off the winter chill with little pots or stews cooked on charcoal braziers.

3 oz. lean pork, cut into thin slices
3 dried mushrooms
oil for deep-frying
10 oz. bean curd, pressed between two plates
for 1 hour and then cut into 1½-inch cubes
cornstarch for rolling
⅓ cup bamboo shoots, sliced
salt and pepper
1 teaspoon sesame oil
MARINADE:
½ teaspoon soy sauce

½ teaspoon rice wine
½ teaspoon cornstarch
¼ teaspoon sugar
SEASONING STOCK:
⅔ cup chicken stock
1½ tablespoons soy sauce
1 tablespoon hoisin sauce
½ teaspoon sugar
THICKENING PASTE:
1 teaspoon cornstarch mixed with
2 teaspoons water

Prepare the marinade first. Mix together the ingredients in a small bowl and marinate the pork slices for 30 minutes.

Meanwhile soak the dried mushrooms in warm water for 30 minutes before discarding the hard stalks and cutting the caps in half.

Mix together the seasoning stock ingredients in a small bowl and leave until required. Mix the thickening paste in a small bowl.

Heat the oil for deep-frying until moderately hot. Roll the bean curd cubes in the cornstarch and deep-fry over moderate heat until they are golden brown, about 4 to 5 minutes. Lift out and drain.

Reheat the oil until hot and deep-fry the pork slices over high heat for 30 seconds, then remove and drain well.

Heat 1 tablespoon oil in a casserole and stir-fry the mushroom and bamboo shoots for 1 minute. Pour in the seasoning stock and add the bean curd and pork slices. Bring to a boil, cover and simmer gently over low heat for 20 minutes. Thicken the stock with the cornstarch paste, season to taste with salt and pepper and serve sprinkled with the sesame oil.

Cantonese Bean Curd Pot

Za Gai Dan Luk Fa
Three Cantonese Scrambled Egg Recipes

Each of these dishes could be served as one dish among others at a dinner. Alternatively, they can be eaten as light snacks with a little plain boiled rice.

Lap Zeung Dan
Chinese Sausage and Eggs

Serves 1

1 Chinese sausage
2 eggs, well beaten
a pinch of salt

1 tablespoon oil
GARNISH:
1 tablespoon minced scallions

Steam the sausage over fast-boiling water for 15 minutes until the fat is running freely. Cut into small dice and mix with the beaten eggs and salt.

In a wok heat the oil and stir-fry the egg and sausage mixture until the eggs are just set. Serve at once garnished with minced scallions.

Note: If using an ordinary skillet use 2 tablespoons oil for each recipe.

Hoi Mei Dan
Dried Shrimp with Eggs

Serves 1

1 tablespoon dried shrimp
1 tablespoon rice wine

2 eggs, well beaten
1 tablespoon oil

Rinse the dried shrimp well in hot water, and drain and soak in the rice wine for 30 minutes before mixing with the beaten egg.

In a wok heat the oil and stir-fry the egg mixture until it is just set. Eat at once.

Tsung Chau Dan
Scallion Scrambled Eggs

Serves 1

---

2 eggs, well beaten
4 teaspoons minced scallions

a pinch of salt
1 tablespoon oil

Mix the beaten egg with the scallions and salt. In a wok heat the oil and stir-fry the eggs until just set. Serve at once.

Note: Salted duck eggs can be used for any of these recipes. This would make the dish more expensive and rather special, and therefore more suitable for a dinner than a snack.

Sam Shik Chau Dan
Egg with Black Fungus and Broccoli

Serves 2

---

4 eggs, beaten
a pinch of salt
oil for frying
1½ tablespoons black fungus
¼ lb. broccoli spears

2 teaspoons minced scallions
1 teaspoon chopped ginger root
1 tablespoon rice wine
1 teaspoon soy sauce
1 teaspoon sesame oil

In a wok or large skillet heat 1 tablespoon oil and pour in the eggs. Season with the salt and gently stir-fry until they are just set. Lift them out and leave to cool on a plate before dividing into 1½-inch pieces.

Soak the black fungus in warm water for 30 minutes. Rinse well, discard any hard bits and pull into small pieces.

Blanch the broccoli spears in lightly salted boiling water for 1 minute and then refresh in cold water before draining well.

In a wok or large skillet heat 2 tablespoons oil and stir-fry the scallions and ginger root for 15 seconds. Add the black fungus and continue stir-frying for another 30 seconds. Add the eggs and broccoli spears. Season with the rice wine and soy sauce, mix well and serve immediately sprinkled with sesame oil.

Ju Yuk Gao
Egg Packages
Makes 12

4 large eggs
4 teaspoons cornstarch
¼ cup water
½ teaspoon salt
¼ cup oil
salt and pepper
STUFFING:
5 oz. lean pork, chopped
2 tablespoons salt pork, chopped
2 teaspoons rice wine
1 teaspoon soy sauce
1 teaspoon finely minced scallions
2 teaspoons cornstarch

SAUCE:
1 tablespoon black fungus
3 dried mushrooms
1 cup soybean sprouts
1 tablespoon oil
1 cup chicken stock
1 tablespoon soy sauce
1 teaspoon sugar
THICKENING PASTE:
1 teaspoon cornstarch mixed with
2 teaspoons water
GARNISH:
1 tablespoon chopped chives

First prepare the stuffing. Pound the pork and salt pork together into a paste as directed on page 25. Transfer to a bowl and beat in the rice wine, soy sauce, scallions and cornstarch. Divide into twelve portions. Set aside.

Beat the eggs with the cornstarch, water, salt and sugar.

In a small 4-inch skillet, or a wok, heat a little oil and put in 1½ tablespoons of the egg mixture. Cook over moderate heat as an omelet until it is almost set. Lift the pan from the heat and put one portion of the stuffing on the egg. Fold over half the omelet to cover the stuffing and press around the edge to seal. Return to the heat for another 15 seconds and then lift carefully out onto a plate. Repeat with the remaining egg mixture and meat stuffing.

Soak the black fungus and dried mushrooms separately in hot water for 30 minutes. Discard the hard mushroom stalks and cut the caps into thin slices. Rinse the black fungus, discard any hard bits; cut the rest into strips.
Mix together the thickening paste in a small bowl.

In a wok or large skillet heat 1 tablespoon oil and stir-fry the black fungus and mushrooms for 1 minute. Add the bean sprouts and stir-fry for 30 seconds before adding the chicken stock, soy sauce and a pinch of sugar. Slide in the egg packages very carefully and cover the pan. Simmer for 15 to 20 minutes. Season to taste and thicken with the cornstarch paste.

Lift packages out on to a heated plate, spoon sauce over them, and garnish with chives.

Egg Packages

Fu Yung Ha Chau Dan
Egg and Shrimp Fu Yung

Serves 2

4 eggs
½ teaspoon cornstarch
¼ lb. boiled shrimp, shelled
¼ teaspoon salt
½ teaspoon sesame oil

1 tablespoon oil
GARNISH:
1 tablespoon minced scallions

Beat the eggs with the cornstarch, add shrimp, salt and sesame oil.

In a wok or large skillet heat the oil and stir-fry the shrimp and egg mixture until it is just set, but still moist. Serve garnished with minced scallions.

Tung Lo Wan Om Chun Dan
Quail Eggs with Cucumber and Straw Mushrooms

Serves 1

6 quail eggs, hard-cooked and shelled
oil for deep-frying
1 teaspoon grated ginger root
1½ tablespoons red onion, chopped
½ cucumber, cut into wedges
12 straw mushrooms
SEASONING SAUCE:
¼ cup rich chicken stock

2 teaspoons rice wine
2 teaspoons soy sauce
½ teaspoon sugar
THICKENING PASTE:
1 teaspoon cornstarch mixed with
2 teaspoons water

Deep-fry the quail eggs in moderately hot oil until they are golden-brown, about 2 minutes. Lift out and drain.

Mix together the seasoning sauce ingredients in a small bowl and set aside.

Mix the thickening paste in a small bowl.

In a wok or large skillet heat 2 tablespoons oil and stir-fry the ginger root and onion for 30 seconds. Add the cucumber and straw mushrooms and stir-fry for another 30 seconds before pouring in the seasoning sauce. Add the quail eggs and bring to a boil. Thicken with the cornstarch paste and serve on a heated plate.

VEGETABLES

Cantonese cooking originates from a province where there is an abundance of fresh vegetables growing throughout the year, and much of its character comes from the use of these vegetables in all kinds of dishes. In recent years, thanks mainly to the growing demand for these vegetables in the West, a very large range of vegetables are available, including luffas, fuzzy melons, Chinese spinach and broccoli, eggplant of varying shapes and colors and even fresh lotus root. A Chinese cook has a basic rule of thumb for handling unfamiliar vegetables: green leaves, stir-fry; others, braise or stew. Generally speaking, the quicker fresh vegetables are cooked, the less elaborate seasoning they require. Green-leafed vegetables are usually torn into pieces or cut into short lengths, while vegetable melons, bamboo shoots and root vegetables are cut into slices, matchsticks or wedges.

To cut wedges, hold the knife at an angle and rotate the vegetable through 90° between each cut.

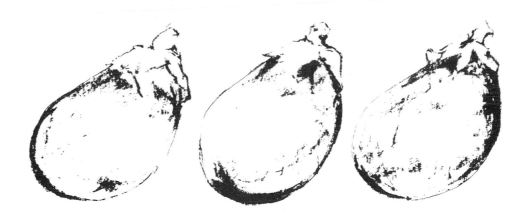

Shi Chap Cheung Fu Gua
Stuffed Bitter Melon with Black Bean Sauce

Serves 1

1 light-colored fresh or canned bitter melon
cornstarch for dusting
STUFFING:
6 oz. ground pork
½ tablespoon beaten egg
1 teaspoon soy sauce
1 teaspoon salt
1 teaspoon rice wine
1 tablespoon cornstarch

1 clove garlic, minced
a pinch of pepper
SAUCE:
1 tablespoon oil
1 tablespoon black beans, chopped
2 slices ginger root, chopped
2 cloves garlic, chopped
4 teaspoons soy sauce

Remove each end of the fresh bitter melon, scoop out seeds and spongy pulp and cut into 1½-inch rings. Blanch the rings in boiling water for 3 minutes, then refresh in cold water before patting dry. Dust the inside of each ring with the cornstarch.

Prepare the stuffing by blending the ground pork with the other ingredients into a stiff paste.

Stuff each melon ring with the meat paste and stand upright on a plate. Place the plate in a steamer over boiling water. Steam over fast-boiling water for 45 minutes.

Meanwhile make the sauce. In a wok or skillet heat the oil and stir-fry the black beans, ginger root and garlic for about 30 seconds, then add the soy sauce and ¼ cup water. Bring to a boil, remove from the heat and keep warm.

When the melon is soft, remove from the steamer. Drain off any cooking juices which may have collected on the plate and spoon over the hot black bean sauce. Serve.

Variation
You can use cucumber in place of the bitter melon.

Stuffed Bitter Melon with Black Bean Sauce

Loeng Pun Chik Gua
Cold Bottle Squash

Serves 1

This recipe is almost identical to one from the north of China in which eggplant is cooked in place of the melon.

1 lb. bottle squash
¼ teaspoon salt
1 tablespoon light soy sauce
SAUCE:
1 tablespoon sesame oil

2 cloves garlic, crushed
1 tablespoon grated ginger root
2 tablespoons light soy sauce

Wash and cut the gourd into four quarters. Place them in a bowl in a steamer over fast-boiling water and steam until the gourd is soft, about 20 minutes. Remove from the steamer and sprinkle with the salt and soy sauce. Leave to cool before paring and cutting into 2-inch pieces.

Meanwhile make the sauce by heating the sesame oil in a small pan over moderate heat. Gently stir-fry the garlic and ginger root for 1 minute, then stir in the soy sauce. Pour the sauce over the squash and mix well. Chill before serving.

Keung Heung Hsuin Gu
Ginger Mushrooms

Serves 1

3 tablespoons oil
1 scallion, finely chopped
6 oz fresh button mushrooms, wiped and with their stalk ends trimmed

½ tablespoon ginger juice
1 tablespoon light soy sauce
1 teaspoon sesame oil

In a wok or large skillet heat the oil and stir-fry the scallion for 15 seconds. Add the mushrooms and stir-fry until they are soft, about 5 to 6 minutes. Add the ginger juice and soy sauce and stir-fry for a few more seconds before serving sprinkled with the sesame oil.

Ung Tsoi Tso Dai Ha
Water Spinach with Shrimp

Serves 2

¼ lb. raw shrimp, shelled, deveined and
   chopped
oil for deep-frying
1 lb. water spinach, washed, trimmed and cut
   into 2-inch lengths
salt

MARINADE:
1 teaspoon rice wine
2 teaspoons egg white
1 teaspoon cornstarch
a pinch of salt

Prepare the marinade first. Mix together the ingredients in a small bowl and marinate the shrimp for 30 minutes.

Deep-fry the shrimp in hot oil for 30 seconds, then drain well.

In a wok or large skillet heat 2 tablespoons oil, put in the shrimp, then the water spinach and stir-fry for 2 minutes. Add ¼ cup water and boil gently until the water has almost evaporated and the stalks of the water spinach are no longer tough, about 4 minutes. Season and serve at once.

Note: If you cannot buy water spinach, use ordinary spinach for this dish; it is different, but good.

Bok Tsoi Chau Ha Mei
Bok Choi with Dried Shrimp

Serves 1

2 tablespoons dried shrimp

2 tablespoons oil
½ lb. bok choi

Place the dried shrimp in a pan of hot water and bring to a boil. Boil for 3 minutes, leave them to soak for an additional 15 minutes and drain.

Meanwhile wash the *bok choi* and tear the bunch into separate leaves, discarding any that are wilted. Cut the leaves into 1½-inch lengths.

In a wok or large skillet heat the oil and stir-fry the dried shrimp for 30 seconds. Add the *bok choi* and stir-fry for another minute. Add about 1 tablespoon water, cover the wok and cook for 2 minutes, before removing the lid and stir-frying for 1 minute. Serve hot.

Lo Hon Sou
Arhat's Fast

Serves 1

This is a modern version of a traditional Chinese Buddhist dish.

⅔ cup cashew nuts
oil for deep-frying
2 slices ginger root
2 scallions, minced
⅔ cup bamboo shoots, cut into ¾-inch pieces
¾ cup red or green pepper, seeded and cut into ¾-inch pieces
8 water chestnuts, sliced in half
¾ cup carrots, parboiled and cut into ¾-inch wedges
¾ cup asparagus tips or broccoli florets, parboiled

salt to taste
1 teaspoon sesame oil
SEASONING SAUCE:
1 tablespoon soy sauce
1 tablespoon sugar
1 tablespoon rice vinegar
1 tablespoon water
THICKENING PASTE:
½ teaspoon cornstarch mixed with
1 teaspoon water

Deep-fry the cashew nuts in hot oil over moderate heat until they are golden-brown, lift out and drain well.

Mix together the ingredients for the seasoning sauce in a small bowl. Mix the thickening paste in a small bowl.

In a wok or large skillet heat 1 tablespoon oil and stir-fry the ginger root and scallions for 15 seconds. Add the bamboo shoots, red pepper, water chestnuts and carrots and stir-fry for 2 minutes. Mix in the seasoning sauce and bring to a boil. Add the cashew nuts and the asparagus tips and season to taste with salt.

Thicken with the cornstarch paste and serve sprinkled with sesame oil.

Ching Chau Kai Lan Tsoi
Stir-fried Chinese Kale

Serves 1

½ lb. Chinese kale
2 tablespoons oil
1 tablespoon rice wine

a pinch of sugar and salt
1 teaspoon sesame oil

Separate the leaves from the central core. Cut the leaves into 2-inch lengths. Pare the hard skin from the central core, and any other stalks which seem very tough, and cut them into 2-inch lengths. Keep the leaves and stalks separate.

In a wok or skillet heat the oil and stir-fry the kale stalks for about 1 minute before adding the leaves to the pan. Continue stir-frying until the stalks are tender, about 3 minutes. Add the rice wine and season to taste with sugar and salt. Sprinkle the sesame oil over the dish and serve at once.

Fa Choi Wui Yuk
Cauliflower with Pork

Serves 1

½ lb. cauliflower separated into florets
2 tablespoons oil
1 scallion, cut into ½-inch lengths
2 oz. lean pork, sliced
salt and pepper

SEASONING SAUCE:
3 fl. oz. rich stock
2 teaspoons soy sauce
2 teaspoons rice wine
THICKENING PASTE:
1 teaspoon cornstarch mixed with
2 teaspoons water

Boil the cauliflower in lightly salted water for 4 minutes, then refresh with cold running water and drain well.

Mix the ingredients for the seasoning sauce in a small bowl. Mix the thickening paste in a small bowl.

In a wok or large skillet heat the oil and stir-fry the scallions for 15 seconds. Add the pork and stir-fry for 1 minute before adding the cauliflower. Pour in the seasoning sauce, bring to a boil and cover the pan. Simmer for 2 minutes. Season to taste with salt and pepper, thicken with the cornstarch paste and serve.

Ho Yau Choi Sam
Choi Sam with Oyster Sauce

Serves 1

½ lb. choi sam
4 cups rich chicken stock

1 tablespoon hot oil
3 tablespoons oyster sauce

Wash and trim the *choi sam* stalks, but leave them whole. Tie the *choi sam* loosely in a bundle with the stalk ends together.

Boil the chicken stock and drop in the bundle of *choi sam*. Cook until just tender, about 2 minutes, then lift out and drain well. Arrange on a heated platter and remove the string. Spoon on the hot oil and the oyster sauce and serve at once.

Sin Bao Choi Tsung
Cellophane Greens

Serves 1 to 2

½ lb. fresh Western spinach, remove central
   ribs and cut into matchstick strips
3½ fl. oz. vegetable oil
3 tablespoons sesame oil

DIPPING SAUCE:
3 tablespoons light soy sauce
1 tablespoon red vinegar

Prepare the dipping sauce first. Mix together the ingredients in a small bowl.

In a deep saucepan heat the two oils together until they are very hot. Put in a handful of the spinach strips and immediately lift the pan from the heat. Stir-fry the spinach for 30 seconds, then lift out on to paper towels to drain. Return the pan to the heat before putting in another handful of the spinach. Repeat until all the spinach is cooked. Serve hot with the dipping sauce.

The spinach can be cooked in advance and reheated when required in a moderately hot oven (375°F).

Heung Mei Wun Dau Gap
Stir-fried Snow Peas

Serves 1

---

2 tablespoons oil
1 clove garlic, crushed
2 slices ginger root, chopped
1 small dried chili pepper

½ lb. snow peas, topped and tailed
salt
1 teaspoon rice wine

Heat the oil and stir-fry the garlic, ginger root and dried chili pepper for about 15 seconds. Remove the chili pepper. Add the snow peas and stir-fry for 30 seconds. Pour in 1 tablespoon water, cover the pan and simmer for 3 minutes. Remove the lid, season with salt, add the rice wine and serve.

Hoi Mei Sin Choi
Stir-fried Celery and Soybean Sprouts with Dried Shrimp

Serves 1

---

1 tablespoon dried shrimp
oil for deep-frying
1¼ cups celery, cut into 2-inch matchstick
   strips
2½ cups soybean sprouts, trimmed

1 tablespoon chicken stock
½ tablespoon soy sauce
½ teaspoon sugar
salt

Place the dried shrimp in a pan of hot water and bring to a boil. Boil for 3 minutes, then leave to stand in the water for 15 minutes. Drain well. Deep-fry the shrimp in hot oil for 30 seconds. Lift out and drain well.

   In a wok or large skillet heat 2 tablespoons oil and stir-fry the celery and bean sprouts for 1 minute. Add the chicken stock, cover the pan and simmer for 2 minutes. Remove the lid, mix in the dried shrimp and season to taste with soy sauce, sugar and salt. Serve at once.

Quail Eggs with Cucumber and Straw
Mushrooms (page 60) and Stir-Fried Celery
and Soybean Sprouts with Dried Shrimp

SOUPS

There are two kinds of Chinese soups: family and formal. A family soup is thin and is basically a hot drink to go with the meal rather than a separate course. It can almost always be made very quickly at the last moment. Many simple stir-fried dishes can be converted into soups by adding a stock and adjusting the seasoning.

Formal soups are quite a different matter. They are usually made with thickened stock and often contain either a large range of different ingredients or expensive ingredients. They may also take a long time to prepare. The soups served in restaurants are always formal.

The order in which a soup is served in a meal depends on the kind of soup it is. Obviously a soup that is a drink will be served with the other dishes at the beginning of the meal but if beer, for instance, is being drunk with the meal, then the soup can be served at the end to refresh the palate. A formal thick soup, will always be served as a course apart from other stir-fried dishes, usually after the small dishes are finished.

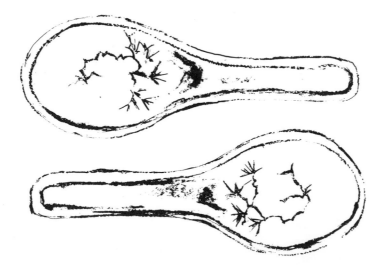

Sou Choi Dau Fu Tong
Bean Curd Vegetable Broth

Serves 4

Silk bean curd is like junket and breaks as soon as it is touched. Handle it, therefore, as little as possible and cut it just before adding it to the soup.

1 tablespoon black fungus
2 tablespoons oil
1 cup chicken, cut into thin strips, ½ inch ×
*   1½ inches*
1 tablespoon rice wine
2 teaspoons light soy sauce
4 cups rich chicken stock
⅔ cup bamboo shoots, cut into strips ½ inch
*   × 1½ inches*

15 snow peas, topped and tailed and cut in
*   half diagonally*
salt and pepper
1 package silken tofu
THICKENING PASTE:
1 tablespoon potato flour mixed with
2 tablespoons water

Soak the black fungus in warm water for 30 minutes. Rinse well, discard any hard bits and tear into strips.

Mix the thickening paste in a small bowl.

In a wok or large saucepan heat the oil and stir-fry the chicken strips for 1 minute. Stir in the rice wine and soy sauce before pouring in the stock. Bring to a boil and add the bamboo shoots, snow peas and black fungus. Thicken the soup with the potato flour paste and season to taste with salt and pepper.

Finally cut the bean curd free from the package on to the palm of your hand. Carefully cut it in half lengthwise and then into ¼-inch thick slices. Slide the bean curd into the soup, bring back to a boil and serve.

Dung Gu Tong
Clear Winter Mushroom Soup

Serves 4

2½ cups dried mushrooms
1¼ cups warm water
2½ cups chicken stock
2 teaspoons chicken fat

1 teaspoon sugar
1 slice ginger root
1 scallion
1 teaspoon soy sauce
salt and pepper

Soak mushrooms in the warm water for 30 minutes, discard the hard stalks.

Place mushroom caps, soaking water and remaining ingredients in a casserole. Seal the pot tightly and steam for 2½ hours. Remove scallion and ginger root and skim off the surface oil. Season and serve at once.

Choi Hung Sin Yu Tong
Rainbow Fish Soup

Serves 4

---

6 oz. haddock fillets
4 dried mushrooms
4 cups well-seasoned chicken stock
2 oz. (⅓ cup) cooked shrimp
½ cup tomato, skinned, seeded and chopped
  into 1-inch pieces
6 tablespoons bamboo shoots, cut into 1-inch
  wedges

¾ cup snow peas, topped and tailed and cut in
  half diagonally
3 slices ginger root
2 teaspoons rice wine
salt and pepper
THICKENING PASTE:
2 tablespoons potato flour mixed with
3 tablespoons water

Dip the fish into boiling water for about 1½ minutes. Cut the flesh into 1-inch pieces.

Soak the dried mushrooms in warm water for 30 minutes, then discard the hard stalks and cut the caps in half.

Mix the thickening paste in a small bowl.

Bring the stock to a boil and add the fish, shrimp, tomato, mushrooms, bamboo shoots, snow peas and ginger root. Bring back to a boil, and add the rice wine. Season to taste with salt and pepper and simmer for 2 minutes. Mix in the thickening paste and serve at once.

Rainbow Fish Soup

Sz Gua Dan Tong
Luffa and Egg Soup

Serves 4

---

2 tablespoons oil
1 lb. small luffas. Pare off the hard ridges and
    cut into wedge-shaped pieces

4 cups rich chicken stock
2 eggs, beaten
salt and soy sauce

In a wok or saucepan heat the oil and stir-fry the luffa wedges for about 30 seconds. Add the chicken stock and simmer until the luffa is soft, about 5 minutes. Season to taste with salt and soy sauce. Trickle in the beaten eggs and serve.

Variation

A more expensive and, therefore, prestigious soup, can be made by substituting 1 lb. bottle squash for the luffa and using 2 salted duck eggs.

Fan Ke Ju Gon Tong
Tomato and Liver Soup

Serves 4

---

6 oz. pork liver, cut into thin strips about 1½
    inches long
2½ cups stock
3 slices ginger root
salt and pepper
½ lb. tomatoes, skinned and sliced
MARINADE:
2 teaspoons soy sauce

1 teaspoon rice wine
THICKENING PASTE:
1 teaspoon potato flour mixed with
1 tablespoon water
GARNISH:
1 tablespoon minced scallions

Prepare the marinade first. Mix together the ingredients and use to marinate the pork liver for 15 minutes.

Mix the thickening paste in a small bowl.

Bring the stock and ginger root to a boil and season to taste. Drop in the strips of liver and stir to separate. Add the tomatoes and boil for 30 seconds before mixing in the thickening paste. Serve at once.

Sai Yeung Choi Gai Zap Tong
Chicken Giblet and Watercress Soup

Serves 4

5 oz. chicken giblets (liver, heart and gizzard)
4 cups chicken stock
2 teaspoons grated ginger root
1 teaspoon rice wine

10 oz. fresh watercress, picked over and cut
   into 2-inch lengths
8 canned straw mushrooms
1/2 teaspoon sesame oil
salt and pepper

Trim the fat and hard gristle from the chicken giblets and slice. Blanch them in boiling water for 20 seconds, then rinse them quickly under cold water and drain well.

Bring the stock, ginger root and rice wine to a boil. Add the watercress and straw mushrooms and simmer for 3 minutes. Season to taste with salt and pepper and add the chicken giblets and sesame oil. Return to a boil and serve.

La Choi Ya Gon Tong
Duck Liver and Preserved Vegetable Soup

Serves 4

6 oz. duck liver, sliced
4 cups well-seasoned chicken stock
1 oz. sichuan preserved vegetable, washed
   and sliced
1 red chili pepper, seeded and sliced
salt and pepper

MARINADE:
2 scallions, cut into 2-inch lengths
2 slices ginger root
1 tablespoon rice wine
1¼ cups cold water

Prepare the marinade first. Mix together the ingredients in a small bowl and use to marinate the duck liver for an hour.

Bring the stock to a boil in a saucepan. Add to the stock the duck liver and its marinade. Simmer gently until the liver changes color. Lift out the liver slices, rinse in cold water and set aside. Strain the stock through a clean cloth and return to a clean pan. Bring gently to a boil and skim the surface very carefully.

Finally add the sichuan preserved vegetable and chili pepper to the stock and simmer for 5 minutes. Season to taste with salt and pepper and add the duck liver. Serve at once.

Dau Nga Yuk Si Tong
Soybean Sprouts and Meat Threads Soup

Serves 4

Soybean sprouts have a delicious, slightly nutty flavor and are bigger and more robust than mung bean sprouts. Soybean sprouts are not, however, always available and mung bean sprouts can be substituted.

1 tablespoon oil
5 oz. lean pork, cut into matchstick shreds

½ lb. soybean sprouts, washed and trimmed
1 pint stock
soy sauce, sugar and salt

In a wok or saucepan heat the oil and stir-fry the pork shreds for 30 seconds. Add the bean sprouts and continue stir-frying for another 30 seconds before pouring in the stock. Bring to a boil, cover and simmer for 5 minutes. Season to taste with soy sauce, sugar and salt and serve at once.

Note: If using mung bean sprouts, bring the stock to a boil, season and serve.

Hoi Dai Ju Yuk Bao
Seaweed and Pork Pot

Serves 4

Kelp is very rich in iodine and trace elements but has a strong flavor when it is boiled and, therefore, may not be to everyone's taste.

1 oz. dried kelp
3 oz. lean pork, cut into thin strings
2 tablespoons light soy sauce

¼ teaspoon sugar
½ teaspoon salt
1 teaspoon sesame oil

Soak the kelp overnight in cold water, then rinse well and cut into very thin strips. Place the seaweed in a pan with 4 cups cold water and bring to a boil over high heat. Boil for 10 minutes, skimming the surface of the liquid frequently. Add the meat shreds and stir to see they are well-separated. Season with the soy sauce, sugar and salt, add the sesame oil and serve.

RICE & NOODLES

In southern China the staple for all meals is plain boiled rice; people often eat three or four bowls of rice with their meals. The Cantonese prefer a long-grain variety of rice *(Indica)*, similar to patna rice, but for special dishes and wine-making they use glutinous rice. This has a rounder, whiter grain than ordinary rice and is much stickier when cooked. Short-grain rice is not a suitable accompaniment for Cantonese food. In southern China rice flour is used to make noodles, and flat ribbons of fresh rice noodles called *ho* are sometimes sold at Chinese grocers, as well as dried rice vermicelli. The Cantonese also like wheat flour noodles for one-dish snacks. The sauces and soups which go with these noodle dishes, like so many Cantonese recipes, are very versatile and can easily be varied by adding or subtracting an ingredient according to what is available in the pantry. Most recipes of this kind are not written, but belong to traditional domestic cooking techniques handed down from mother to child. Snack dishes are always served on individual plates.

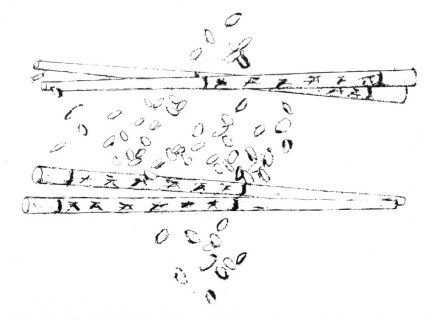

Bak Fan
Plain Boiled Rice

Serves 4

---

2 ½ cups long-grain rice, washed in several   3½ cups water
baths of cold water

Put the rice into a pan with the water and bring quickly to a boil. Reduce the heat, cover the pan and boil gently until all the water has evaporated, about 20 minutes. Turn the heat to the lowest possible setting and with the lid firmly on, leave the rice to steam for 10 minutes. Turn off the heat and leave the rice to dry for an additional 15 minutes before serving.

Gai Fan
Chicken Rice

Serves 2

---

3 cups rich chicken stock   1 cup long-grain rice, well washed and
4 chicken wings, each cut into four pieces   drained
3 slices ginger root

Bring the chicken stock to a boil in a pan or casserole and add the chicken wings and the ginger root. Simmer for 5 minutes skimming the top of the stock as the scum rises. Then add the rice and return to a boil. Reduce the heat and cover the pan. Simmer until the stock has been absorbed by the rice and then lower the heat to the lowest setting and continue to cook with the lid on for another 10 minutes until the rice is dry, about 30 minutes cooking time in all. Serve on two individual plates.

Note: This dish can be cooked in the oven if required, as follows:
Bring the rice and the stock with the chicken wings to a boil and then pour it into an ovenproof casserole. Cover with a close-fitting lid and cook in a moderate oven (350°F) for 40 minutes.

Sin Gu Chau Fan
Chicken Threads Fried Rice

Serves 2

Cooked rice for frying is better if it has been allowed to dry out completely in the refrigerator overnight before being used. Always store cooked rice in a covered container in the refrigerator.

½ lb. chicken breast, cut into matchstick
   strips
oil for deep-frying
2 tablespoons thinly sliced onion
1 cup rice, cooked with the grains separated
   and any lumps broken up
2 tablespoons frozen green peas
2 eggs, beaten

MARINADE:
1 tablespoon egg white
1 teaspoon cornstarch
SEASONING SAUCE:
½ teaspoon salt
¼ teaspoon sesame oil
¼ cup unsalted chicken stock

Prepare the marinade first. Mix together the ingredients in a small bowl and marinate the chicken threads for 20 minutes.

Meanwhile mix together the ingredients for the seasoning sauce in a small bowl. Deep-fry the chicken in hot oil for 30 seconds. Lift out and drain.

In a wok or large skillet heat 1 tablespoon oil. Stir-fry the onion for about 2 minutes until it is transparent but not browned. Add the rice and the chicken threads and stir-fry for about 30 seconds before adding the seasoning sauce and the peas. Stir until the pan is dry and then mix in the beaten egg. Stir-fry until the egg is set, adjust the seasoning and serve.

Note: For this recipe it is better to use unskimmed chicken stock with the chicken oil still in it.

Bat Yuk Nim Mei Gai
Lotus Leaf Glutinous Rice

Serves 2

The leaves used in this recipe are not eaten but give the rice a fragrant flavor.

½ lb. glutinous rice, well-washed and soaked
  for 1 hour in cold water
1¼ cups water
4 teaspoons lard
a pinch of salt
3 dried mushrooms
¼ lb. boneless chicken breast, shredded
¼ lb. lean pork, shredded or 2 oz. each raw
  lean pork and Cantonese roast pork (page
  16)
2 raw shrimp, shelled and deveined
3 lotus leaves

vegetable oil
SEASONING SAUCE:
⅔ cup mushroom soaking water
2 teaspoons soy sauce
2 teaspoons rice wine
1 teaspoon sugar
1 teaspoon grated ginger root
¼ teaspoon black pepper
THICKENING PASTE:
1 teaspoon cornstarch mixed with
  2 teaspoons water

Drain the rice and put it with the measured water into a pan. Bring to a boil, cover the pan and boil gently until the rice is soft and the water absorbed, about 20 minutes. Mix in 1 teaspoon lard and the salt and leave to cool.

Meanwhile soak the dried mushrooms for 30 minutes, then discard the hard stalks and cut the caps into strips. Reserve the water used for soaking.

Mix together the seasoning sauce ingredients in a small bowl and set aside. Mix the thickening paste in a small bowl.

In a wok or large skillet heat 3 teaspoons lard and stir-fry the meat, shrimp and mushrooms for 1 minute. Pour in the sauce and bring to a boil. Boil for 3 minutes and then thicken with the cornstarch paste. Cool.

Place the lotus leaves in a large pan of boiling water for 3 minutes to soften, then spread them out flat and pat dry taking care not to tear them. Cut away the hard vein at the center of each leaf. Paint each leaf with a little vegetable oil. Make an intact round leaf, by laying one leaf on top of another.

Divide the rice in half and pile one half on to the center of the lotus leaves, flatten the rice into a mound, roughly ¾ inch × 4 inches × 3 inches. Spoon the mixed meat and sauce on to the center of the mound of rice and cover with the remaining rice. Fold over the lotus-leaves, not too tightly, to make a neat rectangular package. Place on a plate with the seam underneath and steam for 40 minutes. Serve hot and unwrap the parcel at the table.

Yifu Noodles with Chicken and Bean Sprouts (page 85)
and Lotus Leaf Glutinous Rice

Long Ha Tong Mien
Soup Noodles with Shrimp

Serves 2

½ lb. raw shrimp, shelled and deveined
¼ lb. haddock fillets or other white fish, cut
   into small pieces
3 dried mushrooms
½ lb. dried flat egg noodles
6 slices ginger root
½ lb. fresh green vegetables as available:
   choi sam, watercress, spinach or snow peas,
   trimmed and cut into 2-inch lengths
4 cups rich stock

salt and pepper
MARINADE 1:
1 tablespoon egg white
1 teaspoon rice wine
2 teaspoons cornstarch
a pinch of salt
MARINADE 2:
1 tablespoon egg white
2 teaspoons cornstarch
a pinch of salt

Prepare marinade 1, mixing together the ingredients in a small bowl. Marinate the shrimp for 30 minutes.

Mix the ingredients for marinade 2 in another small bowl and marinate the fish for 30 minutes.

Soak the dried mushrooms in warm water for 30 minutes, then discard the hard stalks and cut the caps into quarters.

Put the noodles into a large saucepan of lightly salted boiling water with 2 slices of ginger root and boil until cooked, about 4 minutes. Drain and place in fresh very hot water until they are required.

Put ⅔ cup stock in a small saucepan with the shrimp and fish. Bring to a boil and remove the scum as it rises to the top.

In another large pan bring the remaining stock to a boil with 4 slices of ginger root. Add the green vegetables and the dried mushrooms. Return the stock to a boil and add the shrimp and fish mixture. Simmer for 2 minutes and season to taste.

Drain the noodles and divide them between two large soup bowls. Ladle in the soup with the shrimp and green vegetables and serve at once.

Note: You can serve a small dish of chili sauce as a dip with this soup.

Yi Fu Mien
Yifu Noodles with Chicken and Bean Sprouts

Serves 2

---

3 oz. boneless chicken breast, cut into
   matchstick shreds
2 dried mushrooms
½ lb. dried round noodles
oil for deep-frying
2 scallions cut into ¼-inch lengths
2 slices ginger root, shredded
1 slice ham or lean unsmoked bacon cut into
   thin strips
⅓ cup green pepper, cut into thin strips

1 cup bean sprouts, trimmed
salt and pepper
MARINADE:
½ teaspoon rice wine
½ teaspoon soy sauce
½ teaspoon cornstarch
SEASONING SAUCE:
⅔ cup chicken stock
1 tablespoon rice wine
½ teaspoon cornstarch

Prepare the marinade first. Mix together the ingredients in a small bowl and marinate the chicken shreds for 30 minutes.

Soak the dried mushrooms in warm water for 30 minutes, then discard the hard stalks and cut the caps into thin slices.

Meanwhile, mix the seasoning sauce ingredients in a small bowl.

Boil the noodles in lightly salted water until they are soft, about 3 minutes, and then drain well. Divide into two equal portions.

Deep-fry in hot oil each portion of noodles separately until they are lightly colored. Drain well on paper towels and keep warm.

In a wok or large skillet heat 2 tablespoons oil and stir-fry the scallions and ginger root for 15 seconds. Add the chicken and ham and stir-fry for 30 seconds before adding the mushrooms, green pepper and bean sprouts. Stir-fry for another minute and then pour in the seasoning sauce. Bring to a boil and season to taste. Arrange the fried noodles on two heated plates and spoon the stir-fried mixture on top.

SNACKS & SWEETS

Social eating is a great Cantonese pastime – the better the meal, the better the occasion – but even a snack is a time for relaxation and conversation with one's friends. Snacks in Canton range from intricate pastries and dumplings to pots and noodle dishes. In Hong Kong there are many small street stalls selling savory snacks and noodle dishes, where the diners sit at tables arranged on the street.

There are also huge restaurant palaces devoted to the preparation and consumption of more sophisticated dumplings and savory pastries, including *cha siu bao*. Chinese meals, unlike Western ones, do not end with a sweet dish or dessert. Traditional Chinese sweets are very sweet to most Western palates. Most Cantonese sweets and cakes are eaten as snacks between meals and in the evenings, although at big banquets it is traditional to serve a sweet soup and perhaps some sweet pastries towards the end of the meal.

In some family meals sections of peeled oranges, pomelos or wedges of watermelon, depending on the season, may finish off the meal, but this is not traditionally Cantonese.

Cantonese Roast Pork Buns (page 89),
Wuntun Noodle Soup (page 88)
and Crystal Wood Ears (page 91)

Wun Tun Tong Mien
Wuntun Noodle Soup

Serves 2

This is a very popular one-dish snack meal in Hong Kong and southern China.

12 wuntun skins
6 oz. dried flat egg noodles
2½ cups rich chicken stock
1 teaspoon rice wine
1 teaspoon sesame oil
1 cup green vegetables as available; spinach,
   choi sam, *watercress, trimmed to*
   2-inch lengths
salt and pepper to taste
FILLING FOR WUNTUN SKINS:
¼ cup ground chicken

¼ cup ground pork
1 water chestnut, ground
½ teaspoon minced onion
½ teaspoon grated ginger root
1 small clove garlic
¼ teaspoon rice wine
¼ teaspoon cornstarch
¼ teaspoon sesame oil
a pinch of salt and pepper

Prepare the filling for the wuntun skins first. Mix the ground chicken and pork with the remaining ingredients for the filling and blend thoroughly.

To fill a wuntun skin, hold it flat on the palm of one hand with one corner of the skin pointing towards the finger tips. Place one teaspoon of the filling in the center of the skin. Fold the fingers down over the palm of the hand tightly to bring one half of the skin over the filling. Move the thumb across the palm of the hand pressing firmly to fold the left-hand corner of the skin over to the right. Place the folded wuntun on a plate and repeat with the remaining wuntun skins. Set aside until required.

Drop the noodles into boiling water and boil for 4 minutes. Lift out, drain and store in fresh hot water until required.

Put the stock, rice wine and sesame oil in a saucepan, bring to a boil and add the green vegetables. Allow to cook for about 2 minutes. Adjust the seasoning to taste.

Bring to a boil a large pan of water and drop in the wuntun. Boil until they rise to the surface, about 3 minutes. Lift out with a slotted spoon and drop them into the stock and green vegetables.

Drain the noodles and divide between two heated soup bowls. Ladle the wuntuns, green vegetables and soup over the noodles and serve.

Guang Sik Cha Siu Bao
Cantonese Roast Pork Buns

Makes 6 buns

DOUGH FOR BUNS:
1½ cups all-purpose flour
2 teaspoons baking powder
1½ tablespoons lard
¼ cup sugar
3½ fl. oz. warm milk
flour for dusting
6 squares of waxed paper, about 3 inches

FILLING FOR BUNS:
6 oz. Cantonese roast pork, see page 16, cut
*   into ½-inch cubes*
SAUCE:
1 tablespoon sugar
½ tablespoon cornstarch
1 tablespoon soy sauce
1 tablespoon hoisin sauce
3 fl. oz. water
½ tablespoon sesame oil

Prepare the sauce first. In a small pan mix the sauce ingredients and boil gently until the mixture is thick and syrupy. Mix in the filling of diced roast pork and set aside.

To make the bun dough, sift the flour and baking powder into a bowl and rub in the lard. Mix in the sugar and then add the warm milk. Mix to a soft dough. Dust your hands with flour and shape the dough into a cylinder. Cut into 6 equal lengths. Roll one length into a ball between the hands, then flatten it into a disc about 5½ inches in diameter. Try to leave the center of the disc thicker than the edges.

Holding the disc of dough in one hand, put a generous tablespoon of the prepared filling in the center of the circle. Gather the edge up around the filling and pinch tightly to seal. Place the round bun, sealed side down on a square of waxed paper. Repeat with the remaining five portions of dough. Cut a cross in the center of each bun and steam over fast-boiling water for 25 minutes. Serve hot.

Note: These buns can be frozen and reheated in a steamer.

Ching Dan Go
Chinese Steamed Sponge Cake

4 eggs
¾ cup sugar

1 cup all-purpose flour, sifted

Beat the eggs and sugar together until the mixture leaves trails across the top of the surface. Fold in the sifted flour. Spoon the mixture into a 7-inch cake pan lined with waxed paper and put it into a steamer over fast-boiling water. Make sure the lid of the steamer is tightly fitting. Steam for 50 to 60 minutes, occasionally topping up the water in the steamer. Serve warm, cut into squares.

Ma Tai Lok Go
Water Chestnut Gelatin

Serves 4

2¼ tablespoons potato flour
6 tablespoons sugar
1 scant cup water

12 water chestnuts, coarsely grated
1 tablespoon lard

Mix the potato flour and sugar together and then gradually stir in the water, taking care to prevent any lumps forming. Stir in the grated water chestnuts and leave the mixture to rest for 30 minutes.

Melt the lard in a saucepan and pour in the water chestnut mixture. Cook gently over low heat, stirring continuously until the mixture thickens and just comes to a boil.

Pour the mixture into a shallow greased dish and steam over boiling water for 25 minutes. Leave to cool for a short time before serving cut into squares.

Note: This gelatin can be made the day before and reheated in the steamer just before it is served. It should always be served warm.

Beng Tong Ngan I
Crystal Wood Ears

Serves 4

½ oz. wood ear mushrooms
10 oz. crystal sugar
4 cups water

GARNISH:
red cherries and *mandarin oranges*

Rinse the wood ears and soak in hot water for 30 minutes. Tear the fronds apart and discard any yellow or hard bits.

Dissolve the crystal sugar in the measured water over low heat. When it has dissolved, bring the syrup to a boil. Strain this syrup through a clean cloth.

Put the wood ears and the sugar syrup into a bowl and steam over boiling water for 1 hour.

Allow the sweet soup to cool, then chill well. Garnish with the cherries and mandarin oranges.

Hang Yen Cha
Almond Tea

Serves 4

The standard recipes for almond tea are often rather complicated. This simple recipe, coming from a domestic Cantonese cookbook, is simple to prepare.

1¾ cups boiling water
¼ cup ground almonds
½ cup sugar
1¼ cups cold milk

THICKENING PASTE:
2 tablespoons potato flour mixed with
2 tablespoons water

Prepare the thickening paste first. Mix together the ingredients in a small bowl.

Mix the boiling water with the ground almonds and the sugar and bring to a boil. When the sugar has dissolved, stir in the cold milk and the thickening paste. Heat very carefully, stirring continuously so that the mixture thickens but does not boil and form a skin. Serve warm.

Variation
For a stronger almond flavor add ¼ teaspoon almond extract.

CANTONESE MEALS & MEAL PLANNING

Cantonese food, even at a family meal, is a social affair with all the family sitting together around the table. A standard family meal is made up of four dishes, soup and plain boiled rice. If the family is large, the dishes are made larger, while for an unexpected guest, an additional dish is quickly added. Everyone has a pair of chopsticks, a rice bowl and a soup bowl as well as small bowls for any dipping sauces. All the dishes are put on the table together and using their chopsticks, people help themselves from each dish as they please. The thin soup serves partly as a drink with the meal, and people ladle it into their soup bowls whenever they wish. The rice bowls are constantly refilled.

A larger, more formal dinner is usually eaten in a restaurant or at least cooked by professional chefs who are hired for the occasion. Such a dinner often starts with four quickly cooked small dishes served all together, followed by a big formal soup, a whole bird or large piece of meat and a whole fish, each served as a separate course. A sweet soup followed by fried rice or noodles might be served after the fish. Plain boiled rice can be served with the meal or not as the host chooses.

Choosing the dishes

It is quite easy to adapt Cantonese domestic and restaurant systems to your own family's kitchen and mealtimes. The central idea behind the choice of dishes is the interest created by variety and contrast. Choose recipes which provide a wide range of different textures, tastes and colors. Always think of the meal as a whole. If you choose one recipe from the meat chapter, then select the others from the fish and seafood, birds, eggs and vegetable chapters. Try to arrange that if one dish has shreds another will have bigger pieces of food. A meal with all of the food one color is as dull as a meal with only one sauce. Vary the flavors of the dishes between sweet and sour, garlicky, chili-hot or salty and bitter, but take care not to have too many overpowering flavors in one meal or you may knock out everyone's sense of taste. Choosing different methods for cooking each dish also adds to the interest of the meal and can lighten the job of the cook.

It is probably easier when it comes to choosing particular recipes to settle for one, which you like to cook or is a family favorite, and then select the other three dishes to blend and contrast with the first.

Planning the cooking

Always remember that while in a traditional Chinese family there are many family members or servants to help prepare and cook a meal you are probably on your own. Most people, when cooking in the Chinese style, find themselves pressed for time at the end of the cooking phase. Try to arrange for one cold dish, or one that can be cooked well in advance, and choose one steamed dish or a slow cooked braised dish which will not need last minute attention. A recipe with a thickened sauce can always be kept warm in the oven for a few minutes after it is finished without doing it much harm. Ideally, leave yourself only one stir-fry which will need last minute cooking. Also bear in mind the limitations of your stove: do not arrange to cook five dishes when you only have four rings. An electric rice cooker and a deep-fryer can both be of great help. Some dishes, particularly braised and slow cooked ones, can be made in advance and then deep-frozen to be reheated in a microwave oven or on the stove when required. Avoid freezing dishes that have a lot of garlic or onion in them. Freezing and reheating a stir-fry is not usually satisfactory.

Preparing the food

Although many Cantonese dishes only take a few minutes to cook, their preparation does take time and there are no shortcuts when it comes to mixing marinades and sauces, and cutting up meats, ginger roots and scallions. Always allow yourself enough time for these often unfamiliar routines. It helps to follow the Chinese custom of collecting all the ingredients for one dish as they are prepared on to one plate, so there is less danger of confusion in the final cooking. Try out a few recipes for yourself before embarking on a full scale Chinese meal.

A SIMPLE CANTONESE MEAL FOR TWO

Pork with Ginger and Choi Sam (page 23)

●

Lemon Chicken (page 33)

●

Tomato and Liver Soup (use half quantity) (page 76)

●

Plain Boiled Rice (page 80)

All the dishes served together

A CANTONESE FAMILY MEAL FOR FOUR

Cantonese Roast Pork (page 16)

●

Cantonese Curried Chicken (page 34)

●

Stir-fried Snow Peas (page 70)

●

Egg and Shrimp Fu Yung (page 60)

●

Chicken Giblet and Watercress Soup (page 77)

●

Plain Boiled Rice (page 80)

All the dishes served together

A MEAL FOR GUESTS, SERVES SIX

Shun Dak Duck (page 37)

•

Barbecued Spareribs (page 20)

•

Sea Bass with Ginger and Onions (page 41)

•

Water Spinach with Shrimp (page 65)

•

Plain Boiled Rice (page 80)

•

Clear Winter Mushroom Soup (page 74)

Serve the first four dishes with the rice and then serve the soup separately at
the end of the meal.

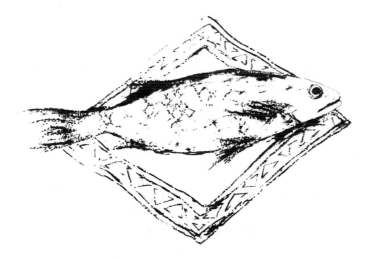

INDEX